Not Ready for Granny Panties

The ~~10~~ 11 Commandments for Avoiding Granny Panties

by Mary Fran Bontempo

Published by eBookIt.com

ISBN-13: 978-1-4566-0929-0

It happens to the best of us. On a day like any other,
you look in the mirror and find a cranky, worn-out,
middle-aged woman staring back at you. A woman
who is firmly strapped into a giant pair of
GRANNY PANTIES.

Yes, aging is inevitable,
but looking, and acting, like your grandma is not.
So join **Mary Fran Bontempo** and learn a new
set of Commandments that will enable you to
avoid the Granny Panties and love life in the
middle years. You'll laugh, learn a few things and
with any luck, bid a permanent goodbye to
GRANNY PANTIES *and* the old hag in the mirror!

Not Ready For Granny Panties

The ~~10~~ 11 Commandments for Avoiding Granny Panties

By: Mary Fran Bontempo

With Illustrations by
Pat Achilles

About *Not Ready For Granny Panties*—The Blog

Several years ago, I found myself surfing the internet in search of a place where I could find content geared towards me—a middle-aged woman who didn't feel, or particularly want to act, middle-aged. I was looking for fun stuff, interesting stuff that wasn't trying to "inspire" me, jam a message down my throat or remind me of the endless array of physical ailments and their "solutions" that came with aging.

In fact, I wanted to avoid the term "aging" at all costs. If I needed to be reminded that I was no longer 20, all I had to do was look in a mirror. Reading about it ad nauseam on the internet was not on my "to do" list.

I also was looking for a site that wouldn't give me a migraine with a thousand links on which to click, fourteen drop down menu items per page heading and a dizzying array of things that flashed, beeped or talked to me without any initiation on my part. (Just try and find the stop button on those videos that start automatically.)

You know what? The pickins were mighty slim. So I decided to start my own site, a place where women like me could go and just have a few minutes of fun every day. A place where I could talk about things that made me laugh, as well as movies, food, fashion and anything else that just made me feel good.

That's how the blog, **Not Ready For Granny Panties,** was born. Along with the help of some really smart, wonderful women (fellow bloggers and friends Pat Achilles, Chrysa Smith and Carmen Ferreiro-Esteban), I developed a site (www.notreadyforgrannypanties.com) just for us—and for you.

Girls just wanna have fun, and we *NRFGP* bloggers realized through sharing with readers that none of us was ready to put on the big bloomers and consign ourselves to Granny Panties, either literal or figurative. As we brought our take on life to *NRFGP*, we realized that there was more to say, about life in the middle and how we can live it to the fullest as the fabulous, glorious creatures we are.

This book is the beginning of that "more to say." I'm certain other things will follow, as I've never been known to let anything go gently. But I also think that at this point, gentle isn't going to get me, or you, where I want to go, which is as far away from a pair of Granny Panties as possible.

So after you've finished the book, remember to stick with us and check out the blog at www.notreadyforgrannypanties.com every day for a daily dose of fun and to celebrate life in the middle with "girls" just like you!

For Dave, David,
Laura and Megan,
who inspire me every day.

Table of Contents

Introduction

It happens to the best of us.

One particular day, a day that starts like any other, you look in the mirror and see someone else staring back at you.

She looks sort of familiar, but you don't quite recognize her, until it hits you with such force that your knees buckle and you think you're going to throw up.

You are staring at a cranky, worn-out woman who looks far older than her years. A woman who looks like fun has become a four-letter word. A woman who looks like (get out a paper bag before you hyperventilate) your grandmother and happens to be you.

Maybe it's the gray hairs seizing control of your head. Perhaps it's the wardrobe that has devolved into a uniform of t-shirts and sweats accompanied by ratty gym shoes and topped off by a pilled cardigan. It might be the lines on your face that suddenly remind you of a roadmap to Hell.

But more likely, it's just a feeling, of invisible, gnarled hands clutching at you and trying to wedge you firmly and completely into a pair of... GRANNY PANTIES.

Actually, you might already be wearing Granny Panties, both literally and figuratively. Literal Granny Panties are just that—panties that your granny would wear. You know the ones; they cover your entire butt, half of your thighs and rise up to just beneath your boobs. That's a horror story in itself, but it's not what we're here to talk about.

We're here to talk about the figurative Granny Panties, the ones which are as much a state of mind as a pair of oversized bloomers. The Granny Panties that keep us from being, and having, FUN.

Women of a certain age are like the Lost Boys from Peter Pan, only not boys and a lot older. Once we hit life's middle ground, society starts to ignore us, occasionally swatting at us like a swarm of annoying gnats hovering on a sweaty summer afternoon.

We're the Lost Women, the ones who've crossed over into marketing "no man's (or woman's) land," having just exited the golden 18-49 year old demographic. We're the women who don't care what a "tweet" is. The ladies who have spent so much time taking care of everyone else that we've forgotten how to take care of ourselves. The women who feel like we're being left behind. And in some ways, we are.

America's fascination with youth has really thrown us under the bus. (It doesn't help that more than a few of us look like we've been run over by a bus. Really, ladies, put on some lip gloss.) Society courts youth. When we cross that line into, well, let's call it, "non-youth," we land on the Island of Misfit Toys, cast-offs in a world that no longer knows exactly what to do with us. We're social and marketing pariahs, which is ironic as our entry into "non-youth" is precisely when we have both the time and money to indulge in things in which we've long been interested but haven't had an extra moment to explore.

That's why it's so important to resist. To link arms with your hot flashing sisters and set fire to the notion that just because we're a certain age, we're irrelevant. You don't have to be relegated to the sidelines of your own life. You don't have to be ignored. And you don't have to be forced into Granny Panties, morphing into a real-life version of the cartoon character, Maxine, and grumbling your way through your days. (Although adding some "Maxine Moxie" to your attitude can be a healthy addition to your behavioral repertoire.)

Women stuck in Granny Panties are caught in the rut of always taking care of someone else and believing their best years are behind them. It just isn't so. At least it doesn't have to be. Avoiding the dreaded Granny Panties doesn't take a lot of time or money. It simply takes a willingness to invest in yourself, change your attitude and for God's sake, throw out any shirt with an animal on it.

But it's not all about appearance. Ultimately, being "Not Ready For Granny Panties" has little to do with face lifts, tummy tucks or dressing like your teenage daughter. It's a whole lot easier than that. A few simple adjustments and some commitment to yourself, for a change, will lead you to a whole new world. A world in which every once in a while, you take center stage. Because you deserve it. Because you've earned it. And because you in Granny Panties is something no one, especially not you, wants to see.

Being *Not Ready For Granny Panties* is not about trying to deny your age. It's about living, to borrow Oprah's phrase, "your best life" at exactly the age you happen to be. It's also about not letting that age define you in a negative way. Just because you're over 50 doesn't mean you can't take up surfing. But please don't wear a bikini while you do it. A little common sense (just a little) makes all the difference between being the kind of woman people look at and say, "I wish I were like her," as opposed to "Thank God I'm not like her!"

The march of time is inevitable. We've always been aware that the years were passing, but it's not until the fateful day when we see that barely recognizable woman staring back at us from the mirror that we know we're on the verge of losing ourselves to Granny Panties. Yet the conclusion of time's forward march—that you will end up feeling beat, bored, miserable and trapped in Granny Panties—is not inevitable by any means.

So come with me and learn a new set of "Commandments." They aren't etched anywhere in stone, but they should be. Because if you follow them, you'll renew yourself, you'll learn to enjoy your life and most important, you'll steer clear of Granny Panties, both literally and figuratively.

As for the cranky, old hag in the mirror? With a little work, a little luck and a healthy dose of fun, you may never see her again.

The Players

Me: The occasionally hysterical woman behind this rant against Granny Panties. "I'm mad as Hell and I'm not gonna take it anymore!"

Dave: My frequently bewildered but always indulgent husband, who likely supports me for his own survival, but I'll take what I can get.

Kids: David, Laura and Megan, my children, occasionally maligned, but much loved. Thanks, kids.

My Mom: Same as above.

Chrysa: My partner in crime, blogging and adventure who regularly talks me down off the ledge (or up onto a ledge, depending on our mood).

Women of the Chorus: Maxine, my cousins, my sister—Karen, Dianna, Kakie, Dorothy Gale, Glinda the Good Witch, Miss Gulch—a.k.a. Elphaba, a.k.a. the Wicked Witch of the West, Oprah, Pat, Carmen, Chris—my b.f.f., my grade school girlfriends, Donna—my best friend from college, my hero, Kathy H., and others. Without these ladies, be they real or fictional, life, and this book, would be impossible (or at least a lot less FUN).

The First Commandment:

Thou Shalt "Fuhgeddaboudit"

Tony Soprano was no dope.

A thug, morally reprehensible, perhaps, but not a stooge. For Tony was capable of dispensing priceless advice in a word—"Fuhgeddaboudit."

(Okay, so it's really "Forget About It," but if Tony says it's "Fuhgeddaboudit," I'm not going to correct him.)

Truth be told, that one word (or three, but who's counting?) speaks volumes. Of course, when Tony said it, he was usually advising some guy to forget something he'd witnessed, for the guy's own health and well-being. "Fuhgeddaboudit" or something pretty bad is probably going to happen, at least in Tony's world.

But Tony was on to something, something we women would do well to remember—or forget, that is.

We spend countless hours of our lives trying to remember stuff. Where we have to go, what we have to do, who we have to get where. We remember who said what to whom, when it was said (especially if we're talking to our spouses and the statement in question was made twenty years ago) and the vocal inflection with which it was said. (How many times have you said, "What's THAT supposed to mean?" to a seemingly innocuous statement made by a spouse who immediately regrets opening his mouth?)

We keep mental lists which expand exponentially on a daily basis. And invariably, we forget something—or someone. Ever leave a kid at the orthodontist because you forgot to pick him up after dropping off his sister at her piano lesson, stopping at the bank and fetching the dry cleaning? Come on; you know you did.

Try as we might, we just can't remember it all. Which is the point. We're never going to remember everything; it's useless to even try. (Except for the kid, of course. But he'd find his way home eventually.) Trying mightily and forgetting anyway just sets us up for failure, and really, haven't you had enough of that?

As we get older, Mother Nature tries to drive home the point that attempts to remember everything are futile by stripping our minds like a field for planting—a field on which nothing is growing, that is. In the last week, how often have you walked into the next room with purpose and direction only to forget why you went in there in the first place? Was it once? Twice? Ten times? Or have you forgotten that, too?

Make no mistake; forgetting is the natural order of things. You, at one time or another, are going to forget your middle name, your best friend's phone number and the fact that your youngest child hates tomatoes. You will also forget a plethora of other stuff.

And you know what? It doesn't matter. Because while your kid will register shock and horror that you no longer have the complete itemized list of her likes and dislikes committed to memory as you did when she was small, she is now old enough to remind you that she hates tomatoes. Even better, she's old enough to make her own vegetable for dinner. Further, how important is a middle name, anyway? And check your phone; your girlfriend's number is in there. (If you forget how to look up your contacts, ask the kid who hates the tomatoes. If she's still speaking to you, that is.)

The worst part of all of this forced memorization is that what it also forces you into is a gigantic pair of Granny Panties. Trying to hold onto everything for everyone makes us cranky, miserable and it robs us of time—for ourselves. When you get right down to it, probably ninety percent of what we're trying so desperately to hold onto doesn't mean a thing. So instead of looking at nature's gradual elimination of totally inconsequential information from your head as a sign that the end is near, see it as a passport to personal freedom.

Do you know when your computer crashes and that little message comes up advising you that a memory dump is commencing? Embrace the dump. If your mind is divesting itself of some of its contents, go with it. Let go of anything that's painful, old news or simply not important.

If it has no relevance to the moment at hand, if it doesn't impact your life in any major way, if it makes you miserable to mull it over, turn it loose and Fuhgeddaboudit. As in Tony's world, it can be good for your health. When you de-clutter your brain, you make room for other stuff. Fun stuff. Interesting stuff. Stuff that might even make life more enjoyable.

None of this means that you abandon your actual responsibilities. If it's really important, write it down and slap it on the fridge. (You know you'll end up there at least fourteen times throughout the day; you're bound to see it.) But if it's not essential, if you don't have to take your mother to the gynecologist (Dear God, yes, it's come to that), then forget it.

Forget old grudges. Forget the fact that you were passed over for a promotion five years ago and you still feel the bile rise every time you remember that the boss's nephew got the job. (It's the boss's nephew; of course he got the job.) Stop replaying the argument with your sister-in-law over and over in your head. (If you didn't make that witty comeback, it's too late now anyway.) Forget that the auto mechanic fleeced you and charged you for repairs you didn't need. (You already paid the bill; just don't go back there.)

And for heaven's sake, forget everything that is, or should be, within the realm of your kids' (we're talking adult "children," here) responsibilities. We served as their personal assistants for their entire childhoods. It's time to let them remember their own stuff from now on. Even if you do remember when their school loan payment is due, tell them you forget. If you don't, you'll set a precedent that will have you calling them each month to remind them to pay their mortgage, their electric bill and their internet service bill. (Assuming they ever move out, of course.)

Forget to do the kids' laundry. Forget to change their sheets and clean their rooms. Forget to pick up whatever it was they asked you to get them at the store. Refuse to serve as their personal calendar, recalling when they have to make the next dentist appointment or renew their gym membership. Occasionally, forget to make dinner. Or just buy bread and lunchmeat. Let the bear cubs forage for themselves.

It's also okay to forget where your husband put his keys. Or his phone. Or his briefcase. Or his jacket. Or his favorite tie. It's not that you don't love him, or care about his or the kids' happiness.

It's just that you're not responsible for it. You're not responsible for keeping track of all the things that keep everyone else on track, even though you've set yourself up as the one who steers the ship and all of its minutiae.

While you being the mistress of your domain and its inhabitants is pretty much essential early on, in order to keep your household from bursting into flames, now it's time to "Fuhgeddaboudit" and force, if necessary, everyone to remember their own stuff. It's not about being mean-spirited; it's about independence and self-sufficiency for them, relief for you. And it's time for everyone to move on, whether they like it or not.

Forgetting, not only your own extra baggage, but everyone else's as well, is your key to release, a release that will open your mind, and your life, to new possibilities, ones that are infinitely more engaging than replaying old hurts or recalling when your daughter's car is due for inspection. Forgetting stuff that isn't yours to remember or things that you shouldn't bother remembering, will also keep you out of a nasty pair of Granny Panties. Freedom for your head, freedom (figuratively) for your bum.

So pay attention to what Mother Nature and Tony Soprano are trying to tell you. Forgetting can be good for your well being. If you must remember something, again, write it down and put it up on the fridge. If you can remember where you keep the paper and pens, that is.

Try This!

Below, list ten things that you think you "have to" remember to take care of this week. After you've completed the list, review it and cross out anything that is really someone else's responsibility. Then, "Fuhgeddaboudit!" and inform the masses that they'll have to remember their own "stuff" from now on.

1._____

2._____

3._____

4._____

5._____

6._____

7._____

8._____

9._____

10._____

Next, write down five things that you've been holding on to—old grudges, hurts, perceived failures—anything that makes you feel lousy but is no longer an active part of your life. Then, review the list...and CROSS OUT EVERY ITEM. In other words, "Fuhgeddaboudit!" once and for all.

1._____

2._____

3._____

4._____

5._____

Now, while we're on the subject of forgetting...

The Second Commandment:

Thou Shalt Ignore More

It's not often that I'll give our male counterparts the nod in leading the way towards a more peaceful existence, particularly given that, if it weren't for the men in our lives, peace might not seem like a foreign word to the majority of women. (Sorry, guys, but you do have a way of stirring things up.)

But when it comes to ignorance, I'll admit, the guys have it. Men are experts at ignoring, and as a result, ignorance, a term which, although maligned, is really quite ingenious.

Before the fellas commence howling at the insult, hear me out. Ignoring more is a clear path to an unperturbed, serene life. Ignoring the majority of life's bedlam makes for an outlook that remains steady, unaffected by emotional upheaval. Men are masters at tuning out emotional upheaval. Unless it involves a sporting event, you'll rarely see a man with his Granny Panties in a bunch.

Consider the following scenario, which no doubt played out countless times in your home when your children were young. A kid is on the phone talking to a friend, with dad three feet away at the kitchen table. At some point, the kid says, "Wait a minute; I'll go ask my mom," at which time the child proceeds to scream "Mom!" at the top of his/her lungs to ask permission to "go to so-and-so's house, see a movie, have people over, etc."

Mom, wherever she is (usually in the bathroom), responds by screaming, "What? What do you want? I can't hear you! What is it?"

Following ten minutes of shrieking, communication finally ensues, the question is answered, and everyone returns to the order of business as usual. Everyone, except, of course, dad, who has yet to stray from business as usual, or from the newspaper he is reading at the kitchen table. Dad, employing his expertise at ignoring both his screaming child and shrieking wife, has remained dedicated to his own pursuits, unperturbed by the goings-on around him.

Men develop this expertise early on in life, beginning as young boys, when they conveniently "don't hear" ninety percent of what their mothers tell them. Studies have been done which maintain that men genuinely cannot hear many tones in the female vocal register, a claim to which my husband has clung desperately since we met. This "fact" has allowed men everywhere to regularly employ what my husband has come to refer to as the "Sergeant Schultz rule."

Sergeant Schultz was the notoriously dense German soldier in charge of policing a wily bunch of World War II prisoners in the 1960's sitcom *Hogan's Heroes*. Colonel Hogan and his crew continually undermined the Germans' operations by spying, intercepting German plans, and spiriting prisoners to freedom. Through it all, Sergeant Schultz would seemingly miss the machinations taking place directly under his nose, all the while proclaiming, "I see nothing. I know nothing," in a clipped German accent.

While we women have spent our lives consulting experts, comparing personal strategies with our friends and reading instructional manuals on everything from child-rearing to how to handle our in-laws, our husbands have spent their lives studying the behavior of one Sergeant Schultz.

When the kids were young, Dave rationalized that whatever his response to a kid-posed query, mine would likely contradict it. He recognized that had he granted permission when permission should have been denied, general mayhem would have ensued and he would have found himself at the center of a maelstrom—thus, the activation of the Sergeant Schultz rule. If he sees nothing and knows nothing, he must therefore remain blameless before God and men, or more important, me.

Although I claimed to be exasperated by his routine, the truth is I was, and remain, envious of his cluelessness, be it actual or affected. If only I could ignore the goings-on around me instead of inserting myself into every situation within earshot. How I wish I could say, "I see nothing. I know nothing," and mean it.

But I can, and so can you. My cousin, Valentina Bartolomeo, she of the wisdom born of South Philadelphia, has another way of putting it: Mind your own business. Once, while attending a family function, a relative cast a disapproving look at "Valli," who was smoking a cigarette. In a manner unique to South Philly Italians, one that admonishes, but with a rough hug, Valli looked directly at the offended party and said, *"Mind your own business!"* as she continued to smoke, unperturbed. Case closed.

Remember the old lady on your street who was always peering out her window taking notes on the indiscretions of the neighbors? Remember how everyone hated that old lady? She wore Granny Panties. And if you want to stay out of them, MIND YOUR OWN BUSINESS.

There are a million small incidents in a day during which ignorance is the ideal response. Those boys walking down the street with their pants hanging down around their asses looking ridiculous? Ignore them; it's none of your business. A commotion taking place at the neighbors across the street? Unless it sounds like someone is getting hurt, pull the shade and stay out of it. Workplace drama commanding undue attention? See nothing; know nothing.

Basically, stop looking for reasons to be offended. Because if you look for them, you're going to find them, no doubt. Then you'll waste precious time stewing over things that really have nothing to do with you. Things that don't actually impact your life in any way, except that once you've internalized them and made them your business, they crowd your mind and sap your energy, leaving you talking to yourself and unproductive.

Further, keep what you know about someone else to yourself. Gossip isn't known as a notorious time-waster for nothing. If you hear a juicy tidbit about so-and-so, keep your mouth shut and *mind your own business*. Put a little of the energy you'd expend hashing out someone else's troubles into creating some joy and fun for yourself. Stay above the fray and ignore the swirling maelstrom on the outside.

Yet external goings-on aren't the only things we should refuse to absorb. Perhaps the most important thing we gals have to learn to ignore is right under our noses and sounds borderline blasphemous: Our kids. Just like dad when the munchkins were small, it's now our duty to turn a deaf ear, or more accurately, a highly selective ear, to their daily demands—for their sakes as well as ours.

It's ridiculously hard to ignore our kids, especially when, from their births, it was our job to protect them and direct their every move. The problem is that we didn't know when to stop, creating a culture of dependent adults who could probably function just fine on their own, if we only let them.

But we don't. Many well-meaning moms (and of course I don't mean me) entwine themselves so intricately into their kids' lives that sometimes we can't figure out where one thread ends and another begins, so we continue to do everything for them well past the time when they should be handling their own stuff. (Okay, I do mean me.)

It would be easy to cast the blame on them and bemoan our notion that they can't live without us, but we created this. And unless we change the status quo, by first getting over our need to be the answer for everything and then gradually extricating ourselves from their daily junk, we're assigning ourselves to a life in Granny Panties, eternally responsible (at least in our own minds) for everyone else, never having time for ourselves, and serving as perpetually whining sacrificial lambs—lambs in Granny Panties.

So, is your daughter fighting with her boyfriend? Murmur sympathetically, nod at appropriate intervals and ignore the entire thing. Odds are, she's venting and anything you say can and will be used against you at a later date anyway.

Is your son failing a class in his major? Tell him to get his act together; let him know he'll have to pay for the class if he flunks, and then mind your own business. It's his problem (provided you stick to your guns and hold him accountable) and he needs to take responsibility for his actions. Are your kids fighting with each other? Tell them to get over it and refuse to hear details. It's highly likely they're all in the wrong one way or another. Married kids having troubles? You really need to stay out of this one. Be empathetic, murmur, nod and repeatedly sing the alphabet in your head until your kid stops talking.

Again, if there's a serious issue, by all means get involved. But generally speaking, sympathy is fine; adding your two cents isn't. Ignore more; mind your own business and let everyone else mind theirs. If you stay out of stuff that doesn't concern you, both outside of your home and in it, you'll have more time for fun or learning something new or even a nice, long nap—the benefits of which should never be underestimated.

I won't say this often, but you've got to hand it to our men and the Sergeant Schultz rule; playing dumb is really pretty smart. See nothing; know nothing, and keep the Granny Panties on the old lady in the neighborhood who is currently peering out her window clucking at the world's misdeeds—and not on you.

Try This!

List five things below that annoy you but really don't affect you in any genuine way. (i.e. men who wear ponytails. Yeesh!) Then, write the phrase "Ignore this!" next to each item. Mentally picture yourself placing each item in a box labeled "IGNORE."

1._____

2._____

3._____

4._____

5._____

Next, list five additional things that you find yourself gnawing on that are none of your business. (i.e. You think your neighbor is fooling around with the mailman.) Next to each item, write "Mind your own business!" Then, do it.

1._____

2._____

3._____

4._____

5._____

Since ignoring more requires loosening your grip (or stranglehold) on your definition of what's important, let's keep moving in that direction....

The Third Commandment:

Thou Shalt Lose Control

What image comes to mind when you think of vacations? Leisurely, relaxing days spent lounging about broken up only by leisurely, relaxing meals followed by more leisure and more relaxing?

Ha! What a waste of time! Vacations aren't for relaxing. Vacations are for cramming in as much fun as a 24-hour period will allow, figuring in a few hours (but only a few—time's a wastin') for sleep. Vacations are for fun, fun, fun, followed by a month of recovery time. I mean, you only get one vacation a year if you're lucky, so what's with all this sitting around? There's stuff to do, folks! Let's get our butts in gear!

Sigh. I confess; I ran our family vacations with the precision of a four star general planning an attack. Disney vacations were the worst, as I had our trips mapped down to the minute, from when we would rise to which park we'd attend on a given day (A different park opens at 7:00 AM for Disney hotel guests, you know), to which ride we'd hit first, to which line we'd stand in when we got to the attraction on the list. (Yes, there was a daily list, and stick to the line on the left. Everyone else always goes right.)

Of course, I'd factor in hotel pool and swim time, followed by showers, dinner (reservations made three months in advance), then back to another park for evening rides, parades and/or fireworks. Everyone back to the hotel, collapse into bed and then rise the following day for more of the same. It was so bad that we actually lost weight on vacations, despite the additional caloric intake.

I wish I could say that my neurotic need to control every second of my (and my family's, God help them) life was limited to annual excursions to Disneyworld, but then Pinocchio and his lying nose would have nothing on me.

I think my neurotic need for control began during my grade school days, when the nuns instructing us in the ways of faith convinced me that life was a fight. A fight against the devil and the world's evils, which would devour me and my immortal soul should I drop my watch for even a moment. (In their defense, every day *was* a fight for them, squaring off against a classroom stacked with 72 first graders. Mortal combat, Catholic school style.)

So, I subscribed to the method of planning out my life ("God helps those who help themselves") and then fighting to adhere to the plan, regardless of how many times it involved banging my head against a wall, slumping to the ground in a semi-conscious state and picking myself up to repeat the entire migraine-inducing process.

As I grew, my efforts at control extended to just about everything, as I not only manipulated my children's day to day lives, but my husband's (after all, I was only trying to "help"), my mother's, my grandmothers', my sister's, my brothers', and any other person's who crossed my path and was foolish enough to ask my opinion about...well, anything.

I did my best to control the past, replaying events and conversations, adding the witty comebacks I should have tossed off during discussions long-since forgotten by everyone but me. I tried to control the present—down to the nanosecond, and I tried to control the future, worrying and planning for as many possible outcomes to a problem or situation as I could manufacture.

With every attempt at strangling life's unfolding, I knit myself another row on a giant pair of Granny Panties.

And you know what? Except for possibly cutting ten minutes off a wait time while standing in line at the Pirates of the Caribbean ride, I didn't really change a thing. Wait, that's not exactly true. I believe that I did change the contours of my face, gifting myself with this giant furrow that now lives on my forehead between my eyes. Otherwise, nada.

I didn't stop my kids, or me, or my husband, or anyone else from making mistakes. I didn't stop tragedies and I didn't cause blessings—except on those occasions when I was sleeping and unable to issue my directives, when I'm sure my family felt blessed indeed.

So now, I've decided it's time to lose control. My new mantra can be summed up in the words scrawled across the sky in green smoke by that most excellent villain, the Wicked Witch of the West:

Surrender, Dorothy.

Although the message was meant to terrify Dorothy and her companions, I think Elphaba may have given the little girl from Kansas some good advice.

Surrender has always gotten a bad rap. It implies weakness, cowardice, laziness. But to me, it now means something else: It means a *real* vacation. One where I don't have to be in charge of everything. One where someone else takes the lead, calls the shots, whatever. One where I get to stop swimming upstream like some demented human version of a salmon. (You do know that those salmon end up dead after all that swimming and flinging themselves up into waterfalls, don't you?)

Now, I believe it's time to surrender to a higher power. Surrender to God, or the Force, or whatever you call that Being who is clearly calling the shots. If you don't believe in a higher entity, then simply surrender to the things that are beyond your control, which translates into just about everything.

Truth is you can save yourself a whole lot of angst, and keep your bum out of Granny Panties, if you give up the fight. (Sorry, Sister Marita Roberts.) Enlightenment, salvation—heck, sanity—can be found in the act of throwing up your hands.

Lest anyone mistake talk of enlightenment and salvation as a sudden awareness of my spiritual nature let me clarify. I'm more than ready to surrender to a higher power, but it's not because I'm enlightened; it's because I'm exhausted.

Life is a runaway train. Most of the time, the best solution is to let the engineer (who is usually not you) drive it. Sure, it's okay to plan. It's important to have goals. But it's also important to note that when God gets a load of most of our plans, He/She has a giggle fit. Because the plan is not up to us. What is up to us is how we deal with the plan as it's set down in front of us.

None of this means that you give up on your life completely. Just give up on all the stuff you can't do anything about anyway. Like whether your kid passes her college chemistry class. Or whether the traffic jam is going to make you late for your appointment even though you left a half hour early just to be on time. Or whether anyone actually shows up for the dinner you just slapped together after getting out late from work, and having to stop at the bank, the cleaners and the grocery store.

Surrender. Give up the ghost. Let go and let God. Use whatever cliché you need to get your head around the idea that everything is pretty much out of your hands anyway.

It's not all about the big stuff, either. Give in to the moment. If you're stuck in traffic, instead of bursting a blood vessel, play around with your radio. Listen to something new—a new song, a different station—and sing along. Loudly. If no one shows for the dinner you made, throw it in the fridge, scoop yourself a bowl of ice cream and turn on some trash TV. If your daughter fails chemistry, she'll take it again, or drop out of school and become a beautician. And that's her call, so turn it over.

Of course, it would be great if once you let go of life's junk and stopped being a raving control freak, God would open all sorts of windows and doors leading to fabulous, life-changing, affirming, wonderful opportunities and blessings. That might happen. But the more likely outcome is that you'll have fewer panic attacks. You'll have fewer migraines. You'll wake up in the morning without a stomach ache. And frankly, that's enough.

Yet, consider the possibility that when things don't go the way you plan, perhaps there's another plan in the works that holds something better. Something more interesting, more exciting, more fun. Or something entirely different, that will reveal a new passion in your life. Maybe it's none of that. Maybe it's the Universe telling you to "Relax! It's all going to work out!" despite whatever you do.

Losing control is actually an illusion, since we don't really have control, anyway. Dorothy and her companions, in spite of their best efforts to avoid any confrontation, ended up in the Wicked Witch's clutches, certain of their own doom, yet ultimately causing the witch's demise, because THAT'S WHAT WAS SUPPOSED TO HAPPEN.

I'm not endorsing the notion that we each have a predetermined life path, but regardless of your best efforts to direct your every move, and the moves of those around you, "Sh*t" happens. When it does, we have little choice but to be flexible and adjust to the surrounding circumstances or risk the aforementioned head-banging and ensuing blackouts.

Surrendering is ultimately an exercise in personal freedom. If you don't control it, you can't be responsible for it. Life isn't supposed to be a battle; it's supposed to be an experience, at least for those of us blessed enough to live where we do and in the circumstances we are. When your back isn't against the wall in a state of personal crisis, don't create one by having a meltdown if your day doesn't go according to plan. And really, aren't you used to that by now? When's the last time your day DID go according to plan?

Of course you've got to initiate some action in your life, otherwise you'd never get out of bed. As tempting as that occasionally is, the real solution is to set up your day and get to it, but BE FLEXIBLE. Get moving, work your plan, but don't have an aneurysm when something throws you off course. (You know it will.) Find an alternative to the meltdown.

Think of detours as opportunities. The truth is, if your higher power wants you to head towards a certain path, you're going to go there, sooner or later, like it or not. So go with the flow and stop swimming upstream.

Here's another analogy: Have you ever lost your purse? A woman without her purse is a woman cut off from mission control in the middle of a firefight. At least that's what it feels like. But no woman has ever died because she lost her purse (unless she was going to pay off her bookie and lost the money, but that's another story). If you lose your purse, life gets a little inconvenient, but eventually, you figure it out. You replace what you need and you probably get rid of a lot junk.

So surrender your metaphorical purse. Relax. Lose control, of your plan and everyone else's. Slip off the Granny Panties and from now on, instead of shrieking "Oh my God!" when life takes a detour, shrug and say, "Oh my God, please take this mess off my hands." Then pour yourself a glass of wine, munch on some expensive dark chocolate and contemplate the metaphysical mystery of it all, right before you change your plan, close your eyes and take another nice, long nap.

Try This!

In the space below, remember the last time you had a meltdown because life didn't go according to plan. Write down the details of the experience— what caused it and how you responded. Then, write down at least three alternative behaviors, things you could have done to surrender to the moment and give up control. Note how the alternatives may have changed your mood and thus the rest of your day. (i.e. A traffic jam makes you late getting home from work. The old you bursts a blood vessel, the new you sings to the radio, listens to a book on CD, calls a friend to catch up—on speaker phone, of course!)

_____

_____

_____

_____

_____

_____

_____

_____

_____

**After you surrender, maybe you'll decide it's
time to lose control another way....**

The Fourth Commandment:

Thou Shalt Do the Wrong Thing

I am so sick of being a good girl.

Be nice. Do the right thing. Think about everyone else in the entire world before yourself.

Initially being "good" meant being safe. "No, no, don't touch, do or play with that" (whatever "that" was), was a prescription for keeping us out of harm's way. Then, it became a matter of keeping others safe around us, as in, "No, no, don't smack your sister; it's not nice."

But eventually, it morphed into, "Nice girls don't do that," again, "that" becoming any number of variables which "good girls" avoided. Nice girls don't wear that. Nice girls don't say that. Nice girls don't think like that. And after a while, the list became so unwieldy that we began running our every thought, action, facial expression, etc., through the arbitrary "nice" rules in our heads, over-thinking everything and afraid to do anything.

Afraid to do anything but expected to do everything.

Did you ever notice how, when something needs doing, the general consensus is, "Oh, just ask so-and-so. She's so nice. She helps out with everything." It's the "nice" women who run the committees, plan the parties, bake the cookies, cook the meals, clean the bathrooms, drive the kids, care for the elders, and on and on and on.

How time consuming. How exhausting. How boring. And ultimately, how impossible.

No one can be good all of the time. We wear ourselves out trying and we fail because it simply can't be done. Then we feel guilty, which makes us think we have to try harder to be good girls. The cycle repeats until we're cranky, suppressed and permanently glued into an enormous pair of Granny Panties.

Well, I've had enough. It's time to be bad. Running with scissors bad. Dye my hair pink bad. Dress entirely in leopard print bad.

All right. Maybe not entirely in leopard print.

The point is, a little "bad" can be freeing. And it can go a long way towards keeping us out of a hiney-pinching pair of Granny Panties. Plus, it can keep our families wondering what the hell we're going to do next. Keep 'em guessing; that's never a bad thing.

Not long ago I decided to take some of my own advice, much to the chagrin of my daughter, who caught me in the act.

"Oh. My. God."

Laura stared horrified at a bandage on my left ankle. "What did you do?!" she gasped.

"What, this?" I asked innocently, holding up my foot for inspection. "Um...that's a dog bite. Yeah, that's right. I got bitten by a little dog when I was riding my bike."

"That's not a dog bite. That's a tattoo! You got a tattoo!" she yelped.

"Hmmm," I mused, studying the fresh bandage. "How about that? Looks like I did get a tattoo."

Earlier in the day, with the encouragement of my friend, fellow *Not Ready For Granny Panties* blogger, Chrysa Smith, I waltzed into a henna shop on the Ocean City, NJ boardwalk and crossed over to the dark side.

With the indulgence of two young girls who were most likely sighing with relief that we were not their mothers, Chrysa walked out with a swirly sun tattoo and I with a flower. Rather, we swaggered out, as life on the edge took hold. And it felt...great. Plus, contrary to what you'd expect, my daughter's horror only enhanced the buzz.

"Are you kidding me? What in the world were you thinking?" Laura asked.

"I was thinking that it might be fun. Everyone's getting tattoos these days. What's the big deal?" I asked.

"The big deal is that you're not everyone! You're my mom!" Laura said.

And there it was. I had committed the unthinkable. I did something decidedly un-mom-like and crossed into naughty territory.

On the scale of badness, it was nothing and being henna, the tattoo disappeared after a few weeks, but the high lasted for a while longer, especially when both my husband and Chrysa's admitted that they found our foray to the other side rather sexy, proving that bad can be very good indeed.

Choosing to be bad intentionally is a thrill ride, before even lowering the bar on the roller coaster. The very act of making a choice to do "the wrong thing" is insanely liberating. Plus, given that for most of us, "bad" amounts to drinking milk directly from the carton, it doesn't take much to indulge in a little grin-inducing naughtiness. The options abound, and if tattoos aren't your thing, don't despair. Being bad, and feeling good, can come in a package as small as four letters.

That's right. Swearing.

My dad was an expert in this field, as are most men. We could tell when my father was in mid-household project as the paint all but peeled off the walls from the heat of his language. But cursing was my father's method of venting. Once it was out of his system, we all moved on.

Swearing has always been an acceptable form of letting off steam for the guys, but hear a woman let loose with a "Son of a bitch!" and you might as well mark her with a scarlet letter.

When I was a good little Catholic girl, I blessed myself and said an Act of Contrition every time I even thought of a bad word, which at the time consisted mostly of hell and damn.

Well, I've learned a few others since then and I can say with confidence that I can swear like a sailor. Before you gasp in horror, I'm in excellent company. None other than Dame Julie Andrews—that's right, Mary Poppins and Maria Von Trapp—has admitted that she can cuss a blue streak with the best of them.

And guess what, girls? It's emancipating. Of course, I'm not condoning walking around in public and letting the F-bombs fly. But when you're having a particularly tough day, a good, hearty "Sh*t!" "God damn it!" and yes, even "F*ck!" screamed at the top of your lungs while safely ensconced in your car, bathroom or bedroom closet can be downright exhilarating. (Yes, I'm sparing those of you with delicate sensibilities, but be assured that as I'm writing, I'm saying the words out loud. Really loudly out loud.)

They're words. Truthfully, they mean nothing. But we've imbued them with such power that it only seems right to allow ourselves to use them to our advantage.

So when life gets particularly stressful, let 'em rip. You can bet your grandmother probably didn't and guess what she wore underneath her clothes?

Yet, it's the pronouncement of an even smaller word that will initially make you feel bad, but then oh so good. In order to stay clear of Granny Panties, you must master the word "NO."

As in, "No, I'm sorry; I can't just throw your clothes in the wash, find your keys, run the church car wash, cook a giant meal for you and your seven friends with an hour's notice, bake a cake for the fundraiser, sell your textbooks on Amazon, spot you your credit card payment, pick you up a sandwich, take your car to the store so I can get you gas, etc., etc." Not that I've ever had to do any of that stuff. I'm just saying.

Sure, we all do little things to help out our spouses, kids and friends. We get involved in causes because we enjoy contributing. But when helping and contributing to other people's lives takes precedence over living your own, you're headed for a boatload of resentment and a fitting for a pair of Granny Panties. You're also on the road to martyrdom—where being nice morphs into being a doormat. Nobody *likes* doormats. They're just a convenient place to dump your dirt.

"Nice" girls finish last, to borrow a phrase. Unfortunately, all too often, having the "nice" label hanging around your neck invites abuse. If you're going to wear that sign, make sure you have its companion—"Feel free to dump all of your crap here because I won't say 'No.'"

Saying "No" may initially feel bad, but take my word for it, when you're sitting on your sofa sipping a glass of wine and reading a book instead of handling everyone else's everything all of the time, it'll feel pretty damn good.

Does all of this mean that you ignore the needs of your family and friends? No, but the operative word is "needs," not stuff they can and should take care of themselves. What it does mean is that you let other people handle their own problems, their own lives and their own stuff. If you can help out when it's truly necessary, have at it. Just don't become everyone else's personal compost heap. It stinks. Literally.

Doing the wrong thing is really a two-fold process. First, refuse to take on everyone else's responsibilities, issues and baggage. Then, embrace getting out of your comfort zone and exploring your own personal "wild side."

Make it an intentional choice to do something "bad." Open your figurative wings and fly over to the dark side for a while. Whatever your version of bad is, (assuming you're a "good girl" at heart and bad for you isn't a secret life as an illegal gun runner), go for it. Dye your hair. Get a tattoo. Pierce something. Have that third glass of wine. Swear a little and say "No" occasionally. You'll also be saying "No" to Granny Panties. (And who knows, maybe "Yes" to a thong. Yikes! Now there's a scary thought.)

Try This!

In the space below, list at least five "bad" things you've thought about doing but never had the nerve to try (i.e. getting a belly button ring). Next to each entry, write down why you think the item is "bad." Then, cross out the reasons why, pick one item (or two, live a little!) and commit to a date and time to DO IT!

Bad thing #1:_____

_____

This is "bad" because:_____

_____

I will do this by:_____

Bad thing #2:_____

_____

This is "bad" because:_____

_____

I will do this by:_____

Bad thing #3:_____

_____

This is "bad" because:_____

_____

I will do this by:_____

Bad thing #4:_____

_____

This is "bad" because:_____

_____

I will do this by:_____

Bad thing #5:_____

_____

This is "bad" because:_____

_____

I will do this by:_____

Next, list five swear words below that "good" girls never say. Pick your favorite, find a quiet, solitary spot, and say the word aloud five times, getting progressively louder each time. Inhale deeply and feel the freedom.

My Favorite Swear Words:

_____

_____

_____

_____

_____

Finally, below, itemize five things you've said "Yes" to in the past when your mind was screaming "Hell, No!" Next to each entry, write down a polite but firm "No" response should you be asked to contribute again. (Just for fun, write an outrageous excuse like, "No, I can't run the bake sale; I'm scheduled to attend an X-rated movie marathon that day.")

1._____

_____

_____

2._____

_____

_____

3._____

_____

_____

4._____

_____

_____

5._____

_____

_____

And although the idea of being a "bad girl"
may frighten you, sometimes scary isn't such
a bad idea after all...

The Fifth Commandment:

Thou Shalt Scare Thyself

Have you read any headlines lately? Terrorism. Economic collapse. Environmental disasters.

It's enough to make a girl crawl into bed, pull up the covers and hide.

The news is scary. Big world, big problems. But that's not all. Your own little world is pretty scary, too. How many times a day does your stomach clench? You know the feeling. The one you get when you think things like, "Are the kids okay?" "Is my job secure?" or "I have a mammogram today." Instant nausea. Instant clench. Instant fear.

Life gives us plenty of reasons to be afraid. It seems as though the potential for disaster lurks around every corner. But when we were young, fear was fun. Remember riding roller coasters? Watching scary movies? Jumping off the high dive? That was scary. And fun. And we couldn't get enough of it.

In some weird way, fear makes us feel more alive. It's why as kids we love Halloween and monsters and ghosts. It's why we hid in closets and jumped out at our friends. It's why we screamed and then dissolved into giggles. We got up close and personal with things that went bump in the night because we knew our parents could keep us safe.

But when we get older we realize that's just false. We start protecting ourselves, playing it safe, doing the cautious thing because that's what grown-ups do. We know all too well the risks of dangerous, scary things and we know that everyday life can offer up something terrifying at a moment's notice, so we water down our lives until we're all drinking skim milk, carrying around little vials of Purel and forwarding every horror story on the internet that involves drugging and kidnapping women in order to "protect" ourselves and our loved ones. (For God's sake, girls, don't park next to that van! Just last week, some cops somewhere found rope, duct tape and a really big knife in a van just like that one!)

How many times did your grandmother tell you not to do something because you might get hurt? How many times did she tell you a story about someone she "knew" who did XYZ and something terrible happened? Granny Panties are big bolts of fabric soaked in fear. Put 'em on and prepare to be terrified of just about everything.

Or, take them off and scare yourself. On purpose.

You don't have to take up bungee jumping or sky diving or extreme cycling. But a controlled thrill is a great way to get your juices flowing again. And it's okay to start small.

Last summer, my husband and I took up kayaking. In the ocean. The ocean is scary. I've seen *Jaws* around a hundred times. Plus, I'm a big baby. Heights scare me. The dark scares me. Wind scares me. The thought of being in the middle of the ocean in something that looks like a giant banana, a mere 18 inches or so from whatever was swimming below, was almost paralyzing.

But our kayaking adventures never took us too far off shore and we only went out on calm days. Still, when I got into the front seat of the thing for the first time and Dave pushed me forward out into the waves, I was terrified. Until, that is, I was thrilled. As the boat jumped over the incoming swells, my stomach lurched while the front of the kayak pointed up to the sky. When it landed back on the water, my view was of nothing but the gray waters of the Atlantic divided by a swath of blue above, the coastline behind me out of sight.

It was exhilarating and peaceful all at the same time. As we paddled in tandem, parallel to the shore, the only sound the blades dipping into the water, I felt stirrings of an excitement I hadn't felt in a very long time. Knowing that I was sitting directly on top of a dividing line between a world of underwater life and my human world was amazing. Sharing it with my husband made it all the more special. Pretty soon the fear was gone, replaced by sheer joy. When we finally returned to shore, riding in with the waves, I couldn't help but whoop with delight.

The possibilities for scaring yourself are endless. If you possess more of a feline sensibility and water sports aren't your thing, try something else. My cousin, Joanna, on a recent vacation with her family, zip-lined her way through a canopy of trees in Hawaii, screaming her head off the whole way down the mountain. She's fifty-four. It's not something she'll work into her daily routine, but taking that leap into thin air made her feel more alive than she had in years.

That's what it comes down to, of course. Taking a leap. A leap of faith that despite being afraid, it's all going to work out. A leap of faith that our fears are just a doorway to a more exciting life. The accompanying screaming is just a form of affirmation. You're screaming so you're obviously alive and letting the rest of the world know it.

Get off the carousel and back on the roller coaster. Can you picture your Granny in a kayak? Of course not. Which is exactly why you should climb into your personal kayak, or fly along on your zip line, or grip the bar in the front car of your roller coaster, or indulge whatever form your fear takes. Fear is exciting. Fear is good. And conquering fear is the best thing of all.

Still, if jumping off mountains or gliding straight out into the ocean is too much to ask, there's another fear that when conquered is just as liberating. The way to conquer it is simple: Sing karaoke.

The fear of looking foolish has stopped every woman dead in her tracks at least once in her life, or more accurately, at least once every day for her entire life. We're so afraid of looking stupid that we miss out on the fun. And singing karaoke is fun.

Who hasn't imagined themselves warbling on stage, microphone in hand, to a throng of adoring fans? You know you have. Except that you probably can't sing. Neither can most folks who climb up on the stage in a bar or club and shriek into a microphone, but it doesn't seem to stop them.

It shouldn't stop you, either. Forcing yourself that far out of your comfort zone will prove one thing: No matter how stupid you look, the world won't end. No one will hate you (except maybe your children but that's a given when you embarrass them) and you won't die.

But you will feel a freedom that you haven't felt in a very long time. A giggle like a kid freedom. A "Who cares, that was fun!" freedom. A "So long Granny Panties!" freedom.

Being silly and uninhibited is a birthright, one that we forget is ours as we age. We don't think of being silly as a scary thing until we become old enough to feel embarrassed, which to most of us is a fate worse than death, or so we think. Yet, acting the fool, when you're in on the joke, is totally liberating and opens up all sorts of possibilities, most of which involve a healthy dose of fun. So sing karaoke, dance like a fool, play hopscotch, do whatever it takes to look stupid. It's one of the smartest things you can do to stay out of Granny Panties.

On any given day, you're going to be afraid. The headlines will be terrible, conjuring visions of the end of the world. Some idiot will turn in front of you in an intersection when you have the right of way, causing a mini-movie of your life to flash before your eyes. Your doctor will call on a Friday afternoon while you aren't home, not leave a message and be out of the office until Monday, forcing you to mentally begin giving away your things.

But remember, terror isn't all bad, especially when it's self-initiated, controlled terror. Fear touches us in a place that makes us appreciate life. No, you can't stop bad things from happening; you can't turn around the economy; you can't stop a tsunami. But you can face your own fears. By scaring yourself on purpose, forcing yourself out of that all-important comfort zone, you embrace feeling alive.

So exhilarate yourself. Get scared, get stupid, and avoid the always terrifying Granny Panties.

Try This!

Make a list below of at least five things that you've been afraid to try (i.e. horseback riding). Next to each item, list the worst thing that could happen if you try each thing. Then, list the worst thing that will happen if you never try any of them. Finally, choose two entries and commit to a date by which you will try and accomplish them.

1._____

_____

_____

_____

2._____

_____

_____

_____

3._____

_____

_____

_____

4._____

_____

_____

_____

5._____

_____

_____

_____

You really should scare yourself. However, if all this scary, stupid fun is just too much at first, there is an easier way....

VI

The Sixth Commandment:

Thou Shalt Regress

It was every kid's fantasy. Each year, the school supplies list went home and always, near the top of the page, there it was: One box of crayons.

And every year, I'd watch enviously as some spoiled kid in class would show up with the one thing I coveted—the 64 crayon Crayola big box of colors.

Oh how I longed to get my hands on Aquamarine, Goldenrod, Lavender and Magenta. And the built-in sharpener? Be still my heart. But it was not to be. Of course I got crayons, but with four school age kids in our family needing supplies, I got the eight pack. Sixty-four crayons were just not in the budget.

To this day, a giant box of Crayolas makes my heart flutter. When my kids were young, it was easy to indulge my passion for crayons, markers, water colors and all things artistic. You can be sure I bought the 64 box of Crayolas. Every Christmas and birthday brought a new slew of art supplies, whether the kids asked for them or not. But as they got older, I had no excuse to purchase my beloved crayons.

The fact is, grown-up toys don't hold a candle to kid toys. Remember Silly Putty? No matter how many times I pressed that elastic dough onto the Sunday comics, the thrill never waned. How about Play-Doh? Was there anything better than opening a fresh container of hot pink dough? What about bubbles? Did you have one of those giant bubble wands? How cool was it to run through the yard trailing an enormous nine foot bubble behind you?

You see, that was never just a box of crayons or an egg of stretchy elastic gunk, or a bottle of dishwashing soap cleverly packaged. That was a box of joy, an egg of creativity and a bottle of wonder. Adult toys, a.k.a. jewelry, cars, computers, etc., are great, but give me ten bucks and a dollar store with a well stocked toy aisle and I'll still grin for a month.

So when was the last time you experienced joy? Carefree, giggle until your face hurts, damn, this is fun, joy? My guess is right around the time you decided you'd outgrown the 64 box of Crayolas and relegated them to the back of the closet. Then you moved onto teenaged angst and drama, right before turning into an adult.

And we all know how much fun that is.

The solution, then, and the way to steer clear of a permanent case of Granny Panties, is to take back your crayons. Yes, girls, it's time to play.

The purest form of play, the one that feeds the soul, is found in the play of children. Think back to how you felt when you pulled out that new crayon, or when you opened the new Barbie, or when you first watched the Slinky walk down the stairs. The smiles, the giggles, the fun.

The problem is that as adults, we don't feel we're entitled to that kind of joy. More important, we've forgotten how to find it. Giggling is something only children or senile old people do. Fun becomes a word harder to define than "hypnopompic," which, by the way, means "Of or relating to the partially conscious state that precedes complete awakening from sleep." In other words, half-asleep—the way many of us are living our lives.

Which is why it's time to go back to the future and perform a little regression therapy.

For starters, hit up that dollar store. They still sell Silly Putty and bubbles. Pick up an egg or two and a bottle of bubbles. Find a few minutes (when no one is around, at least at first, as they'll think you've finally lost it) and just play. Get a newspaper and find a photo of a politician you particularly dislike. Slap on the Silly Putty and distort that face until your heart's content. Blow bubbles and take deep breaths while the breeze carries them up and away. Be a kid again. You'll regress, right back to your happy place.

Buy yourself some crayons (I still highly recommend the 64 pack of Crayolas) and color. If free-hand design is too much too soon, buy a coloring book. In fact, buy one anyway—one with princesses or magic ponies. Color a spot of yellow and then color over it in blue. Rediscover the magic of making green.

Pick up a game of jacks. Sit on the floor (Assuming you can get yourself up again, that is. Otherwise, stick with sitting at the kitchen table.) and test your jacks-playing prowess. Then, challenge your kids to a game. They'll love it and you'll kick their butts, at least until their video game hand-eye coordination kicks in.

The point is, we have to rediscover play and reintegrate it into our lives before we all turn into the old lady on the street who frightens small children. Actually, we'd do well to imitate small children, consciously, before dementia fully grabs hold, and recapture their joy.

It means sacrificing seriousness, which, frankly, is seriously overrated. It means remembering what you loved doing as a kid and figuring out how to do it again in a regular, meaningful way, in your grown-up life. Did you enjoy paint-by-numbers? Take an art class. Were you a basement dancer, spinning records and going crazy with your girlfriends? Sign up for dance lessons, or head out to a restaurant with a good DJ once a month. If you were the athletic type, join a bowling league, a softball team or a walking club. For me, it was all about my bike. And it still is.

Being fully on board with my desire to act like a kid again, my husband bought me a new bike for my fifty-first birthday. (Really, he'd be on board with anything that directs my focus away from him, but I digress.)

This is not just any bike. Nor is it an "adult" bike a la Lance Armstrong, replete with gears and speeds and, heaven forbid, hand brakes. No, this is my six-year-old dream bike, sized and modified to fit my decidedly not six-year-old body.

My new bike is purple, my favorite, six-year-old color, with white daisies on the frame and seat. It sports a white basket set jauntily on the handlebars and most important, it has a bell. The bell is not quite the same as that on my six-year-old bike—it "dings" rather than "brrrings," but, I have a bell on my bike!

The handlebars, set high and wide, let me sit erect on my bike's padded seat (Did I mention that it has flowers on it?!), no hunching over, no lower backache, and I can actually see where I'm going, even look around while I pedal, instead of staring only at asphalt whizzing by.

In fact, on this bike, there is no whizzing; there's only cruising—my bike is a "cruiser," underscoring its purpose. After age fifty, we're all due for a little cruising, especially since the last few years have left most of us feeling like we've been pedaling directly up the side of Mount Everest.

I remember my youthful determination to master a two wheeler. For a six-year-old, learning to ride a bicycle is akin to getting a driver's license. It's the first truly independent form of transportation available to a kid. (Tricycles don't count. A mom can outrun a trike.) Even the symbolism, of a parent pushing a child forwards as the kid wobbles uncertainly before finding her balance and gliding ahead, speaks volumes.

As a child, I knew my bike was my key to freedom. It didn't take me far, just around the block, but while I was riding, my mother never knew exactly where I was. Was I in front of the Reilly's house or just passing the Warren's? Maybe I was at the far end of the street, lingering just a moment and savoring my independence. Either way, I was on my own, with license to explore my world.

It's not much different today. Of course, now I can cross the street, so that expands my territory a bit. But slowing down again and pedaling my way around on a bike takes me back to when a pretty garden would make me stop and literally smell the roses, which I do. I notice things that wouldn't get a second's attention were I in my car. And I love the fact that it's all me, powering, steering and guiding my bike to new horizons. Or maybe just really seeing my horizons for the first time in a long time.

Riding my bike, I'm a kid. And from my perch on my flower-covered, purple seat, everything old is new again. Even me.

Of course you can't turn back the clock. You can't reclaim your youth. But you can reclaim what it felt like to be young, because that joy doesn't have an age limit and it is really the purest form of joy, one that came during the innocence of your youth.

You can't reclaim your innocence, either, not totally. But you can reject the notion that age automatically means you aren't entitled to being even occasionally carefree. You are, even if it's only for a few minutes a day. Which it should be—a few minutes each and every day when you definitively reject Granny Panties and embrace unfettered happiness by doing something you love. Something simple. Something that you discovered when you were a child and still gets your juices flowing. Something that makes you feel like a happy little kid again.

So rediscover the joys of your youth. Buy the Crayolas; pick up some Play-Doh; get a new bike. Go back to the future and bypass the Granny Panties by having a little fun. Regress and rejuvenate. Pretty soon you'll be feeling new again, too.

Try This!

In the spaces below, list five things you enjoyed
as a child. Review each item and choose two or
three that you can still do, no matter how silly.
Then, indulge your inner child and go for it!
(Give yourself a gold star if you write your
answers in crayon!)

1._____

2._____

3._____

4._____

5._____

Next, review the list above. Look at each item
and decide how your childhood joy can be
turned into an adult experience that you can
integrate into your life as a regular source of fun.
Write a corresponding adult experience in each
space below to match your childhood joys above.
Be sure to indulge at least weekly in the adult
version of your childhood fun.

1._____

2._____

3._____

4._____

5._____

Finally, get out your crayons and color in each cartoon in this book. Take your time and add fashion details, accessories, background images, etc. Experiment with different color combinations. In short, be a kid again and just have fun COLORING!

And just to keep you in the "everything old is new again" mindset...

The Seventh Commandment:

Thou Shalt Avoid Mirrors

It happened again this morning.

I woke up, stumbled to the bathroom and found some old lady in there with me while I brushed my teeth.

I don't know how she gets in there, and I don't see her while I'm peeing. She's damn persistent though, showing up every day as soon as I look in the mirror, refusing to leave until after I've showered, dried my hair and performed the daily spackle and paint job on my face. Then, somehow, she slips away, only to return again the next morning.

Lately, though, I've seen her around a lot more. I think she's stalking me. It's the oddest thing; the old bat seems to have a thing for mirrors. Every time I happen by one, there she is, scaring the crap out of me to the point where I've taken to avoiding reflective surfaces of any kind.

The thing about this broad is she looks like she wants me in Granny Panties. And I'm just not going.

Okay, it happens. That day when we look in the mirror and we see (Gasp! Hack! Choke!) our mothers or, God save us, our grandmothers looking back at us. It's not that we think our moms or grannies are nasty; we just don't want to look like them. Because they are old. And we refuse to be.

So, obsessing over what we see, we buy into the delusion that we can avoid the process of turning into our mothers by plunking boatloads of money down on lotions, potions, procedures, treatments, make-up, salons, spas—anything that will slow the inevitable metamorphosis.

There's an easier way: Stop looking in the mirror.

I'll admit this is a tough one. At least it used to be. Personally, I was recently caught flipping down the passenger-side mirror in the car a total of five times to check my hair and make-up while my husband drove us to a wedding where we were going to see absolutely every one of our friends. (When I'm driving, I only flip down the mirror two or three times.) I just couldn't bear the thought that I'd look anything less than perfect, or to be more honest, that I had aged as much as some of the people I'd caught a glimpse of at church. Once we got to the reception, my first stop was the ladies' room—to check my lipstick.

Well guess what? I wasn't perfect and I had aged exactly as much as some of the people at church, a given as we were all born in the late, gulp, 1950's.

Mirrors can be friend or foe, but as we get older, they land more often on the mean side of the equation—witness the daily appearance of that old hag in my bathroom. But it doesn't have to be that way. What's the saying? "If you change the way you look at things, the things you look at change."

Of course what stares back at us from the mirror is changing, and we may not like what we see. But when you do find yourself looking at yourself in an old lady mask, instead of seeing lost youth, look and see someone who's not dead yet. Instead of focusing on the gray hairs, be grateful that you have hair—and then, of course, jot down hair dye on your shopping list. Instead of stewing over the wrinkles, look at the laugh lines and try to remember a time when one of them might have been created—right before you rub in the wrinkle cream.

Sure, that sounds like a bunch of Pollyanna bull-crap when you're trying to deny that your face and body are telling you you're a great candidate for Granny Panties. But it can be done. It's all about balance and attitude.

You're not going to throw in the towel and allow Medusa to have her way with you; I'm an avid student of what's new on the anti-aging front, cosmetically, fashion-wise etc. Just don't obsess over what the mirror is throwing back in your direction.

The way to proceed? Do your morning prep work. Slap on the lotions, potions and make-up. But please, please don't overdo it. Nothing ages a woman like make-up overload. And for God's sake, make sure nothing is smudged and that you color in between the lines with lipstick. Only crazy old ladies can't figure out where their lips are. Fix your hair. Spritz on something that smells lovely. I said "spritz," not drown yourself in a sea of scent. Old ladies can't figure out when to stop spraying, either. Then, take a look in the mirror at what you've created and WALK AWAY.

For the remainder of the day, limit the number of times you check yourself out to cursory glances when in the restroom and pit stops at mid-day and before dinner if you have an appointment. Your goal is to make sure nothing has slid off of your face. Touch up make-up (lightly!), adjust hair and clothes and again, WALK AWAY.

Now, while most of us have an adversarial relationship with our mirrors, there are those who just can't seem to get enough of themselves. You know the ones—the women with the fake hair, fake boobs, fake birth certificates. For them, the mirror is a seductive enemy, but an enemy nonetheless.

Ladies, despite what you think you see in there, you do not look like you're thirty-five. You look like you're fifty-five (or above) trying desperately to hold onto what is no longer yours to keep. It's actually sort of pathetic. If you think you see a thirty-five year old in the mirror, THE MIRROR IS LYING.

Do yourself a favor and follow the advice above: WALK AWAY. Maybe if you can tear yourself away from your own reflection for a while, the illusion will dissipate and you'll return to reality. Believe me, reality won't be nearly as bad as the delusion you've been hanging on to.

If we could turn back the clock by staring in the mirror, I'd have one attached to my forehead and positioned at eye level. But these days, staring in the mirror is more likely to trigger a panic attack and a spike in blood pressure. No one needs that. So don't do it. If the mirror can't be your friend, at least don't turn it into an enemy.

Mirrors should be treated as what they are, a chance for us to see ourselves as everyone else sees us. To that end, we should certainly take advantage of the opportunity to make sure we don't look as though we're auditioning for a part in a horror movie, either by not caring enough or by caring too much (both are cringe-worthy).

But obsessing over what we see keeps us stuck in Granny Panties, whether we're giving up in disgust over what looks back at us, making no attempt to stem the damage, or conversely trying to fool everyone into thinking we're not as old as we are and slathering on enough compound to repoint the brickwork on a house.

Far better to, one day when your pain tolerance is particularly high or you have a bottle of vodka at the ready, stand in front of a full length mirror, sans make-up, Spanx or a perfectly coiffed head, and take a good, long look at yourself.

This is you. This is what you have to work with, like it or not. And if "or not" wins out, then take a few minutes and figure out what you can improve on, short of selling your body to science and scrapping the whole thing.

Do you need a new hairstyle? Call and make an appointment today. Then get online and search hairstyles; some sites will even let you upload a photo of yourself to try on different looks. If you're going gray, make a decision—either hide it or embrace it, and then stop thinking about it. On the other side of the equation, does your hair contain so much product that you could break boards with it? Consider a softer look. Enhance what you've got; don't try and hide what you've lost.

Have you given up on make-up? Try a little mascara, a swipe of lip gloss. It's not overwhelming and will make you look like you give a damn, which you should. If you're adverse to foundation, try a tinted moisturizer. It provides a little coverage and that all important moisture that our middle of the road skin needs. If you put on make-up with a trowel, all of the previous advice applies to you as well.

Last, try and find at least one or two things that you actually like about yourself. It doesn't have to be anything major—maybe you just like your earlobes. Each time you look in the mirror from now on, resolve to look at that part of you first.

Take an unflinching look at what everyone else sees. It's probably not nearly as bad as you think—or as good as you may think (you know who you are). Accept what you see; change what you can, within reason, and then WALK AWAY, acknowledging that there's more to you than what the mirror reflects.

Maybe, just this once, it's not a bad thing to remember that you've earned every little line on your face and buy into some of the Pollyanna bull-crap after all. Free yourself from the mirror addiction and tell the old bag you see first thing in the morning to kiss off; no matter how she tries, she's not forcing you into a pair of Granny Panties. You're better than that, even if she isn't.

Try This!

First thing in the morning, take a look at yourself in the mirror. Make a list of five things you'd change about your reflection if you could. Next to each entry, list one possible, doable solution for what you don't like. (Hate the suitcases under your eyes? Pick up a "de-puffing" eye roller at the drug store. They actually help.) Resolve to try a "fix" for what ails you at least once a week until you've tackled your "to do" list. Then, put the list out of your mind and WALK AWAY from your mirror so you can live your life!

1._____

2._____

3._____

4._____

5._____

Next, keep track of how many times during the day you seek out your reflection in a mirror. List below the number of times and places (the toaster, tin foil, the flip down mirrors in the car) you look at yourself. Resolve to limit your stolen glances to a morning once-over, ladies' room pit stops and an evening face washing. Use the time you save to learn Italian or something.

Hold on a minute. A few more things before we abandon the subject of mirrors...

VIII

The Eighth Commandment:

Thou Shalt Not Wear Elastic-Waist Pants

(or Mom Jeans, or Anything That Makes Your Butt Look Like Two Watermelons Encased in Fabric)

Here's a simple question: How many days a year do we celebrate Thanksgiving?

No, it's not a trick. The answer is one. One single day a year when it is permissible to eat so much that a band of elastic around your waist sounds like a good thing.

Notice I said "sounds" like a good thing. Because although expandable pants might sound like a good idea, unless you are with child (God forbid!) they never, ever look like a good thing.

Okay, I get it. You want to be comfortable. You deserve to be comfortable. But do you want to look as though you've given up? Because that's exactly what elastic-waist pants say.

"Hey, don't mind me. I don't really care what I'm wearing or what I look like. I just want easy. In fact, I'm too lazy to even pull up a zipper, hence the elastic around my waist."

No, you'll never utter the words, but everyone who sees you can hear them as though you're blasting them through a loudspeaker.

If you need another reason to avoid the elastic waist, think of it this way: What did the last pair of pants your mother bought look like? They had an elastic waist, didn't they? All the way around, right? Like I said, we love our mothers and our grannies, but we don't necessarily want to look like them. Put on a pair of elastic waist pants and I'll bet that underneath, the Granny Panties will shortly follow. The day the pants in my closet are the same as the ones in my mother's is the day I pull the shades and start collecting cats. (You know I love you, Mom.)

Elastic waist pants are unforgivable, but for the love of God, don't replace them with Mom Jeans. Just because something is made of denim doesn't make it modern. Remember that *Saturday Night Live* skit in which a group of women donned denim with a twelve-inch rise and elastic around the waist? (Not one, but two horrifying fashion statements.) The ladies bounced around with butt cheeks as big as basketballs, bending over to load stuff into SUVs and mooning the camera with copious amounts of denim. It was hilarious—and cringe inducing.

This is not the reaction you're looking for when you step out of the house, but it's what you'll get if you don the dreaded Mom Jeans.

There are many alternatives out there, and there's not a reason in the world why women can't be comfortable and stylish. As maddening as it is to try and find a pair of jeans that flatter, the fact that there are a million different fits and styles means that there is a brand out there that will work for you, without making you look as though you're ninety or trying to be sixteen.

In fact, you can have your elastic—in your jeans, no less. Spandex is God's latest gift to women, and almost every manufacturer makes jeans with a bit of spandex in them, usually around ninety-seven percent cotton to three percent spandex. The combination allows just the right amount of stretch in the fabric to provide comfort and fabulous fit.

Several companies, like Lee Jeans and Not Your Daughter's Jeans, actually cater to us, wonder of wonders, making pants for women—that's women, not old ladies and not teenage girls. Even discount stores like Wal-Mart and Kmart offer denim lines that can work for women. With the variety of fits and styles available, you may have to spend a little time to find the right pair for you, but you don't have to spend a fortune to look great.

Another no-no that should go without saying yet doesn't, given the number of women strolling the streets looking as though they've just come from the gym, and they haven't—is sweatpants. Sweatpants are for being sick in. Or for snow days. Or for cleaning the bathroom. What they are not for is wearing out in public. They have the word "sweat" in them for heaven's sake.

Ditto the gym sneakers. There's no need for you to be running around in gym sneakers unless you're, well, running around. As in, in a race, or jogging, or actually in the gym. If you can't live without sneakers, buy a cute pair of classic Keds and save the big, clomping gym shoes for workouts.

And while we're listing "No-no's," for the love of God, do not, DO NOT, wear sweaters with reindeer, snowmen, turkeys, pilgrims, Valentine hearts, dogs, cats, teddy bears, Disney characters or anything with the word "Grandma" on it. Should you succumb, know that no one will converse with you about anything other than grandchildren, arthritis and doctor's appointments, a punishment you richly deserve.

Simple, basic tops and sweaters work for everyone. You don't need an advertisement for Disneyworld splashed across your chest. They can market the place without you. Take a long sleeved tee, add a pretty scarf and some earrings—instant, simple style. A tank top or camisole with a long sleeve cardigan on top is comfy and classic. Cozy sweaters are fine, too; just be sure it has some style and you don't look like you're about to burrow underground to hibernate for the winter.

On the other end of the spectrum, don't delude yourself by trying to dress like your daughters. Even if you're slim, fit and attractive, you're not sixteen. Or twenty. Or even thirty. While some basics are transferable, at least in theory, cuts and fits for women differ from those for juniors. If you shop in the Juniors' Department, odds are you're going to end up looking like a Britney Spears wanna-be. And even Britney Spears doesn't want to be herself half of the time.

If you absolutely must wear "comfortable" clothes in public, a pair of good fitting yoga pants (Yes, they have an elastic waist. I'll allow it.), even if you've never transitioned into a downward dog in your life, along with the aforementioned classic long-sleeve tee, a colorful scarf and a pair of ballet flats will keep you pulled together and in the comfort zone. Please, PLEASE, don't wear a matching jacket and pants outfit. Not unless you're on a track team. Stick with black yoga pants and a colored tee. Simple, classic, and the ballet flats call to mind Audrey Hepburn. Who could object to that?

Now for what's going on underneath. I believe undies are a matter of personal preference. That is, I believe thongs are a matter of personal preference. My best friend swears by them. I can't help but think it's like having a piece of dental floss stuck between your butt cheeks.

Regardless, make sure your underwear fits. Go through your unmentionables drawer at least twice a year and get rid of anything with holes, pulls or stretched out elastic. Invest in a few decent undergarments. The fit is up to you, with the caveat that you don't buy undies so large that the band fits above your waist. (These would be the actual Granny Panties we are avoiding.) A woman's waist should be the narrowest part of her torso. Why would you want more fabric around it to make it look bigger?

I'm not suggesting teeny-weeny bikinis; just avoid briefs that reach your boobs. Hipsters are a nice cut; give them a try. But do buy some new things. Not only do you deserve lovely delicates, you'll feel fabulous knowing you're wearing something special, or at least devoid of holes, under your everyday duds.

Oh, and get a bra fitting and buy some new bras. You know your bras are atrocious. We all have unmentionables that are downright unmentionable. Stretched out elastic. Bunched-up cups. And nothing says Granny Panties like seeing the "girls" hanging around your waist while your stretched out bra meets your gigantic underwear. If you have bras in your drawer from the Eisenhower Administration, you probably need a fitting anyway. It's a good bet that the girls, much like the rest of you, don't look exactly the same as they did several decades ago.

Don't assume that because no one can see your undergarments they don't matter. Undies are hardly invisible. With every panty line riding halfway up a butt cheek, every pair of boobs resting around a waistline, you show the world your unmentionables as surely as if you wore them outside of your clothes.

Well-fitting undies, are the foundation (literally) of everything you wear. A good fit means you won't spend the entire day pulling things up or yanking them down. Everything stays where it's supposed to be. Approximately. And that's the best we can do at this point.

Starting with a solid foundation makes it that much easier to follow up with a decent outer layer. You want to look good. It's so much harder to cover nice undies with sweats or Mom Jeans. In fact, I'm pretty sure it's a sacrilege. Your new undies won't allow it and will actually scream in protest.

None of this is rocket science, ladies. It takes minimal time, effort and money to look decent with a few basics. To reiterate the last commandment, we are avoiding mirrors, but not before we at least make sure we won't frighten our neighbors when we walk out the door.

Before you go out in public, try this test: Take one final look in a full length mirror. If you could accessorize your outfit with a can of cleanser and a pair of rubber gloves or free weights, GO AND CHANGE. Further, stretchy elastic bands belong around the heads of babies and little girls, not around your waist. And jeans with a twelve inch rise belong on...well, no one. Dress like a woman, not a girl or a gym rat and treat yourself to some new undies. You'll look better, which always translates into feeling better, which translates into a better day for you and everyone around you.

Give a damn about how you look. Not to the point of obsession—see the previous commandment —but to the point of caring about you. If you don't, no one else will, either.

Try This!

Head to your closet and dressers. With an unflinching hand, remove any and all Mom Jeans, character sweaters, sweatpants and sweatshirts. After perusing the pile, choose two or three pairs of sweatpants and sweatshirts to keep—one for shoveling snow, one for cleaning the bathroom and one for throwing up in. Gather all remaining items—no waffling allowed—and put them in a bag to be donated to Goodwill.

Next, examine your undergarments. Discard any item that has holes, stretched out elastic, bunched padding or is more than four years old. Do not add them to the Goodwill bag. Seriously, throw the crap out.

Finally, use the lines below to list basic items (and colors!) you can and should add to your wardrobe to update your attire and prevent you from looking like your grandmother. Gradually (remember, Target, Kmart, Walmart—it doesn't have to be expensive), replenish the discarded clothing with comfortable, stylish basics and underwear. Remember, you deserve this!

Pants (jeans that fit, yoga pants)

_____

_____

_____

_____

_____

Tops (t-shirts, cardigans, sweaters, camisoles—remember colors)

_____

_____

_____

_____

_____

Undergarments

_____

_____

_____

_____

_____

Shoes (ballet flats, Keds or other stylish sneakers or canvas shoes)

_____

_____

_____

_____

_____

Accessories (scarves, earrings, necklaces, bangles)

_____

_____

_____

_____

_____

Remember, your granny wouldn't buy new undies, which means you definitely should. And as for "shoulds"...

The Ninth Commandment:

Thou Shalt Stop "Shoulding" Thyself

Few words in the English language are better at inspiring dread in women than "should" and its evil twin "shouldn't."

I should do another load of laundry. I should mop the kitchen floor. I should call my sister-in-law. I should go grocery shopping. I should pay that bill. Or, I shouldn't eat that cookie. I shouldn't buy those shoes. I shouldn't say that, think that, do that, etc., etc.

To inspire a whopping case of guilt in any woman you know, ask her what she "should" be doing as opposed to what she is doing, especially if what she is doing is indulging herself in any way. And if she is indulging herself, tell her she shouldn't be. She probably thinks that anyway.

Should and *shouldn't* are our literary jailers. Since we were little girls, those words have been used to control us, and, like so many others, initially with the best of intentions, ostensibly to keep us safe.

You should look both ways before crossing the street. You shouldn't go out alone at night. Eventually, we used them on ourselves, as in, *I should start that term paper early,* or *I shouldn't go out with that guy; he's a jerk.* All well and good.

But somewhere along the line, should and shouldn't morphed into guilt-mongers, making us feel badly about everything we were or weren't doing on any given occasion.

We women run our every thought, action and plan through the "should" filter. Many of the things we "should" be doing aren't even necessary; we've just fallen victim to the idealized fantasy of becoming the perfect wife, mother, daughter, sister, friend, employee, etc., so we try and squeeze in as many "shoulds" as we can to achieve the impossible dream. *I should pick up his dry cleaning, I should get the kids that video game, I should visit my mother.* Inevitably, we fall short, as the list of shoulds is infinite. And irritating. And again, completely impossible to fulfill.

Then, when we go and indulge ourselves to try and let off a little steam, exhausted from "shoulding" ourselves, we invariably crash head-on into the equally infinite list of "shouldn'ts." *I shouldn't have that glass of wine, I shouldn't be sitting here reading, I shouldn't have dessert, I shouldn't spend that money.* And on and on and on.

The uniform for juggling an endless list of shoulds and shouldn'ts? A big, fat pair of Granny Panties.

Try this exercise to get a sense of the futility of this nonsense. Get a piece of paper and start to make a list of all of the things you "should" do. Start with what you should do today and move on to what you should do this week, this month, this year and for the rest of your life. Then compile a similar list of shouldn'ts.

If you're reading again, I assume you've realized how stupid all of this is and put down your pen. Otherwise, you'd still be writing. For the rest of your life.

So here's the proposal. Eliminate "should" and "shouldn't" from your vocabulary. Remove them from your consciousness. Obliterate them from your life, for no good will come of them.

It's like this: "Should" is a synonym for obligation, while "shouldn't" equals denial. The only reason to hang on to them is to preserve a state of martyrdom and misery. If you're into that kind of thing.

We women have been trained to serve as sacrificial lambs for everyone in our lives. We rise in the morning listing the things we have to do for everyone else before we even begin to think about what's going to make us happy. Heck, we generally don't even get to ourselves in a day and when we do, happy rarely enters the equation. When we go to bed, we're back to compiling the list for the next day and again, we're at the bottom.

But if we examine those mental lists without sentiment and without guilt, most of what is on them can be consigned to a "should" or "shouldn't" pile. Things we "should" do for our kids, husbands, parents, employers and so on, followed by things we "shouldn't" do for ourselves because we "should" still be occupied doing stuff for everyone else.

Yet how many of those "should" items could be qualified as a "must"? Likewise, how many of the "shouldn'ts" is an absolute "must not"?

A "must" is an essential, which one has to take care of because if left undone, something really bad could happen. As in *I "must" turn off the iron so it doesn't start a fire and burn down the house*, or *I "must" be respectful to my employer (even thought he's an idiot) so he doesn't fire my ass*, or *I "must" pay my mortgage so the bank doesn't foreclose on the house, forcing me to live in my car in the driveway. The neighbors would frown on it.*

Sounds ridiculous, right? But if you pare down your daily lists to the essentials, the "musts" are actually few and far between. It's not essential that you pick up your husband's dry cleaning. Assuming your kids are grown, it's not essential that you schedule their dentist appointments. Make them do it themselves. It's not essential that you call your mother-in-law if the conversation will make you want to tear your ears off the sides of your head. Tell your husband to call his own mother. Nor is it imperative that you volunteer at church or host every holiday dinner or even mop the kitchen floor every week. (Unless, of course, you're sticking to it; then, a quick wipe-up is probably in order.)

None of these things is wrong in and of themselves. Doing things for others can serve as a balm to our spirits. The danger develops when we take something we "could" do to help someone out and turn it into something we "should" do. Eventually, we create an infinitely itemized list of "shoulds," making us miserable and sentencing us to an oversized, yet oddly pinching, pair of Granny Panties.

The answer, as always, is balance, as well as turning the "shoulds" into "wants." Examine your mental "should" list. Select a few items, absolutely no more than three, that you could easily incorporate into your day, things you "want" to do to assist your family, or friends or co-workers. Then, go for it. Without complaint, without obligation. Then stop. Before you feel that first twinge of "Oh, God," followed by a heavy sigh.

I'm not sure where the expression "Give until it hurts" came from, but it's bull. Give because you want to; give because it feels good, not because you "should" do it. Otherwise, you start to resent the giving, as well as the given-to, and that pretty much negates the whole experience.

More important, remember to give to yourself. All of those things you "shouldn't" do? Like have the wine, relax and read a magazine, eat the chocolate, buy the shoes? Put those things on your "want" list as well. Then do at least two of them, one early in the day, one later, each and every day.

I'm equally unsure where the idea comes from that deprivation and suffering are good. Okay, I'm not unsure at all, it all comes from religion and the idea that because Jesus suffered, we should all aspire to that. At least that's where it comes from when you're raised a good little Catholic girl.

But I don't think we're here to suffer. There's just too much about life that's good and happy and joyful. I'm pretty sure God didn't put all that stuff here so we could look at it and say "Oh, I shouldn't."

Thankfully, at least some pulpit-pounders are endorsing the idea that just maybe, God wants us to have some fun down here. Modern, Bible-based preachers including Joyce Meyer and Joel Osteen encourage us to believe that our Higher Power is one that wants good things for us, so non-stop deprivation is not only unhealthy, it's counter to what God intends. (Meyer even wrote a book entitled *Eat the Cookie…Buy the Shoes*—God love her!)

Needless to say, more rigorous, traditional churches scorn what they consider to be self-indulgence, but I'm a believer. Taking care of ourselves, indulging in an occasional "shouldn't" and limiting the "shoulds" will only lead us to appreciate and enjoy life more, giving us more energy to, as Oprah would say, "Be our best selves," which, to my mind, translates as getting through the day without wanting to run into traffic before the day is over.

Life offers up enough misery and difficulty; seeking it out by mandating our every move and limiting the joy that is readily available is not only stupid, I believe it's an insult to our Higher Power. How would you feel if someone rejected a gift you offered to them? The fact is, if you're reading this book, I'm pretty sure you don't have to walk five miles with a jug on your head to bring back fresh water for your family to survive the day. That is a blessing, one which we need to acknowledge.

I am lucky to be able to sit at this computer and write this book. I'm blessed that my life isn't about survival, but about actually living. There's a reason I was put here, in this country, in these circumstances. Not taking advantage of that is just wrong.

Further, by elevating ourselves and encouraging everyone else in our lives to manage their own stuff, freeing us from an infinite list of "shoulds," we give ourselves the opportunity to contribute to the world in ways that may be exponentially more satisfying —to us and to those who might benefit from our efforts.

Take some of your newfound "should-free" time and do something uplifting. Get involved in a charity you've wanted to be a part of. Teach an adult to read. Learn to play the piano. Sing in a choir. Plant a garden. Do something that makes your life a little better, either by helping someone less fortunate or by adding some beauty to the world.

But do it because you WANT to, not because you should. Take some time and count your blessings. Stop being a martyr. Make your loved ones responsible for themselves; you'll be doing them a favor. Scuttle the "shoulds" and "shouldn'ts"; replace them with "musts" and "wants." Give yourself permission to dump the guilt and balance what you must do with a few things that you want to do. Remember that what you really "should" do is appreciate and experience the joy of your life. What you "shouldn't" do is thumb your nose at the Almighty by ignoring your life's potential.

Refuse to make excuses and burden yourself with the "should" and "shouldn't" lists. Appreciate your life, indulge in opportunity and release yourself from becoming a resentful, overwhelmed wearer of ugly, martyr-making Granny Panties.

Try This!

List below all of the things you "should" do this week. Then evaluate each item to determine if it is a "must" or a "want," writing the word next to the selection. Finally, delegate to a family member or friend any item that is not absolutely within your jurisdiction and proceed to complete your "want to do" list.

Shoulds

_____

_____

_____

_____

_____

_____

_____

_____

_____

Next, list below things you've decided you "shouldn't" do because you think denying yourself is noble. (It isn't.) Next to each item, determine if you could possibly indulge yourself and write down a date and time to do so. (i.e. Read a magazine for 15 minutes daily before making dinner or schedule a manicure.)

Shouldn't(s)

_____

_____

_____

_____

_____

_____

_____

_____

_____

And while you're at it, definitely buy the shoes. Now speaking of shoes...

X

The Tenth Commandment:

Thou Shalt Be Conspicuous

I coveted her shoes.

Even though I knew coveting was a sin (another Catholic rule), I wanted Dorothy Gale's shoes.

Let's return to Dorothy and Oz for a moment and talk about the reason the Wicked Witch had her Granny Panties in a bunch in the first place. If you recall, it was all about the shoes. Rabid desire for those ruby slippers threw the witch into such a frenzy that she launched an all-out attack to get at them.

I can sympathize. Most women have, at some point, been overcome by shoe envy. It starts young. Even at the tender age of seven, I thought those sparkling, sequined, ruby slippers were the most beautiful things I had ever seen.

It was the shoes that made Dorothy special. The shoes that made everyone step back and take notice. And I wanted to be noticed. Somehow, I knew instinctively that a fabulous pair of shoes could do the trick.

But being noticed was not something good girls were supposed to aspire to. When I was young, it was all about blending in, being inconspicuous. We wore uniforms to school. We practiced the Palmer method so our handwriting would all look the same. An inordinate number of us even had the first name of Mary.

After a while, we learned that anyone who dared to be different was suspect. Sameness was safeness and different became synonymous with bad. So I kept my ruby-slippers fantasies, and my desire to stand out, to myself.

As we got older, of course, some girls did stand out: the blond, pretty ones. The ones who dated the football players and cheered for the sports teams. But even those girls had to tow the line and maintain their group's standard or risk being cast out of the popular girl club. Even for the perfect girls, different was bad.

It's no wonder, then, that even as women we strive to "fit in" with whatever group we happen to be a member of at any given moment. We don't want to call attention to ourselves, so we figure out what it takes to fit in at the office, with our neighbors, with the other moms at school, and so on. Then, we tow the company line.

What it comes down to is this: As either girls or women, we do whatever we can to fade into the background. We aspire to be wallflowers. And after a while, we end up looking nothing like Glinda, or even Dorothy. We end up looking like Miss Gulch, a.k.a. the Wicked Witch of the West, pedaling along wearing a permanent scowl and a gigantic pair of Granny Panties.

Yet deep down inside, I'm convinced that there's not a woman in the world who wouldn't jump at the chance to don a pair of those ruby slippers and get off the bike—or the broomstick.

So what's the answer? How do we access our inner Dorothy? Better yet, how do we show off our inner Glinda?

Think for a moment. What is the most festive and adored time of the year? The time when all things excessive, shiny and sparkly are not only the norm, but are encouraged and embraced? Christmas. Even if the holiday doesn't represent your religious persuasion, it's hard not to love the lights, the decorations, the glamor of it all.

Not only do we decorate our living and public spaces during the Christmas season, we allow ourselves to sparkle as well, giving in to indulgences in dress that would have folks staring at other times of the year.

So what's wrong with a little staring?

While I wouldn't advocate regularly dressing head to toe like a Christmas tree, a touch of bright color in your attire can do wonders for your confidence, not to mention your wardrobe. Sure, folks may stare, but being intentionally conspicuous is a thrill ride when you steer the roller coaster.

So in keeping with the Dorothy theme, how about a big girl pair of ruby slippers? Okay, maybe Dorothy's bedazzled version is a bit over the top. But there is an alternative: a pair of red high heels. Nothing will help a woman bust out of a pair of Granny Panties faster than a pair of red stilettos.

I bought my personal pair of ruby slippers several years ago. For the longest time, they sat in my closet, where I would occasionally take them out and try them on with different outfits, standing in my bedroom like a teenaged Cinderella. But I never, ever wore them out in public. That would be too conspicuous.

Until one night, headed out to dinner with friends, I figured, "What the hell?" and I slipped on my red heels with a pair of jeans. It was as though Glinda herself had waved her magic wand and sprinkled fairy dust on my inconspicuous head. Talk about transformative. Those shoes had more mojo in them than the entire population of Munchkinland singing the final chorus of *Ding, Dong the Witch is Dead*.

Was anyone staring? I don't know and I didn't care. All I did know is that I felt different. Confident. Engaging. Dare I say it? Sexy.

You heard right: Sexy. For some reason, we've been conditioned to avoid that word as though it were one of those other four letter words we're not supposed to say. And just like there's nothing wrong with a good cuss word, there ain't nothin' wrong with sexy.

To my mind, sexy doesn't have to equal sex. If it leads to that, ain't nothin' wrong with that, either, but looking great, looking like a woman, looking sexy and being noticed for all of the above is its own reward. (And no, I'm not saying that sex is a reward; for some it's a punishment, but that's a whole other book.)

Choosing to be noticed is empowering. Showing the world that you exist—outside of your defined roles as wife, mother, daughter, etc.—is your right. In fact, it's your obligation. You weren't put here to be a servant, or a shadow puppet, or a modern day Miss Gulch. If you are any of those things in your current incarnation, STOP IT.

Stop letting those roles define you, or at least define all of you. Peel yourself off of your wall and BE CONSPICUOUS. Show the world that you're here. Put on a pair of red high heels, or a leopard print scarf or a pair of dangly earrings.

Throw on an armful of bangles. Wear a hat. Try a bright shade of extra shiny lip gloss.

Smile. Laugh out loud. Dance in public in a flash mob. Dye your hair. Cut your hair. At least comb your hair. Paint your nails purple. Do something, anything, however small, to stop blending into the background.

Being conspicuous can transcend the exterior as well. Put yourself out there by having an opinion. Believe in something and share it. Take a stand on an issue that means something to you. Write a letter to a local newspaper or website on a topic that riles you up—and sign your name!

The possibilities are endless, as are the benefits. By stepping out of your carefully constructed persona and doing something unexpected, you'll not only prove to the outside world that you exist, you'll force those around you to see you in a new light as well. A new light as a person, not as a mother, wife and so on.

Redefining yourself, being conspicuous, will open doors—not only to new experiences and relationships, but to new dimensions within your existing relationships. In short, you'll put some excitement, some fun, back into your life.

And you'll consign Miss Gulch, and her Granny Panties, back to the black and white portion of *The Wizard of Oz*, while you party on with Glinda and Dorothy, proudly showing off your own FABULOUS ruby slippers. You can be the glimmering, glamorous Good Witch, worthy of adulation, which you are.

Try This!

Buy a fashion magazine. (*In Style* or *Lucky* are always good choices.) Take a look at some current trends shown in the magazine. Then, on the lines below, list several items (a leopard print scarf, a shiny lip gloss, etc.) that you can add to your wardrobe to BE CONSPICUOUS! Make it a point to wear at least one item daily that peels you off the wall and makes your look "pop!"

_____

_____

_____

_____

Next, think of at least five ways to be conspicuous that aren't only appearance oriented (writing a letter to a newspaper or commenting on a blog, taking a political stand that your neighbors would hate) and list them below. Choose two items and complete them within the next two weeks. Finish the remaining items within two months. Then continue to add to the list and BE CONSPICUOUS!

_____

_____

_____

_____

_____

_____

_____

_____

_____

_____

**And now for the most important
commandment of all...**

The Eleventh Commandment:

Thou Shalt Engage in Idol Worship

For a number of years now, Americans have been subject to a barrage of television shows which assault the airwaves for weeks on end with questionable "talent" engaged in contests to see who the public will anoint as the next great thing.

While the names of the programs vary, the concept remains the same. Out there, somewhere, is an undiscovered, unappreciated performer just waiting for the world to take notice so she (anyone who has become a bona fide star via this type of programming has been a woman) can take her rightful place as a modern day idol and be showered with the adulation she so richly deserves.

It's contrived, it's ingratiating, it's frequently boring and it's totally unnecessary, especially when the country is full of idols, most of whom rarely receive a "thank you" for making dinner, let alone a recording contract, endless paparazzi coverage and the masses falling at their feet in worship.

Who are all these unsung stars? Well, let's start with you. You, and every other woman who has ever put anyone before herself, which is most of us. If you've ever eaten the burnt toast or the crusts of your kids' sandwiches in lieu of an actual meal, you're an idol. If you've sat up all night watching a sick baby, then worked a full day on no sleep—idol worthy. If you've accompanied an aging parent to multiple doctor appointments, while suffering through endless critiques of your driving skills, you win the prize.

In fact, there are innumerable reasons why almost every woman you know deserves a tiara, a title, a new wardrobe, the car, the money and a tickertape parade. But if you're waiting for a coronation, don't hold your breath. It's not that our efforts aren't appreciated; truthfully, we do our jobs so well that we usually fly under the radar. No one ever really sees us, or what we do to keep the Titanic afloat.

That's part of our role as nurturer and comforter; we do those things naturally and because we want to. We don't expect a reward. Consequently, we usually don't get one.

Most women are far more comfortable as Cinderella in the role of scullery maid than they are as Cinderella as the princess. I didn't say we like the role; we're just used to it. Deprivation becomes the norm, until, that is, we get so overwhelmed by the ever-increasing demands of everyone else that we have a major meltdown, accusing our loved ones of not giving a damn about us, locking ourselves in our rooms and crying hysterically for two hours.

Not that that's ever happened to me. I'm just saying.

Yet everyone knows that a Cinderella in a ball gown dancing with the prince is a far happier Cinderella than the one scrubbing the floors, cleaning up after the mice and waiting in servitude on her rude, ungrateful step-sisters. (Fill in appropriate family members as necessary.)

So put down the mop and bucket and find yourself a ball gown, already.

You see, you, and I, have created this world we inhabit. We've cultivated a climate in which we do everything for everyone else, we fail to expect acknowledgement or thanks for our efforts and then we feel abused and miserable for it.

It's not their fault. It's yours. And mine.

But this isn't a blame game. I'm not giving you one more thing about which to feel guilty. Rather, I'm setting you free. I'm empowering you to make a change because truthfully, this is a fairly easy fix, but you've got to take the reins of your own pumpkin carriage.

The secret is simple: Start treating yourself like a princess and pretty soon, you'll start to feel like one, at least occasionally. And if you're lucky, and consistent with your efforts, folks around you will start recognizing your fabulosity as well.

You don't have to leave home, or let everything and everyone around you go to Hell in a hand basket. You just have to take some time, every single day, to treat yourself well. Plus, you can start by enjoying what's right under your nose.

"I'm saving it for 'good.'" Thus spoke my grandmother when questioned about the curtains, linens and multitude of other items she had carefully stored, out of sight, in her dresser drawers and closets. If an item were "dear," i.e. cost over three dollars, Grandmom saved it, rather than enjoy it in the present day.

When I removed the lovely household items from their hiding places after she passed away at ninety-six, they disintegrated in my hands. Actually disintegrated.

She never used a single one. My grandmother didn't think she was worthy of nice things. In her mind, she deserved to be deprived, and she made sure she was. My grandmother wore Granny Panties —both literal (the proof lay in an unfortunate incident at the nursing home involving my brother, Grandmom and a too-long walk in the hallway, but that's another story), and figurative.

How many beautiful things do you own that you have sitting on a shelf? Or worse, hidden in a closet? Remember that china you received as a wedding gift? How many times have you eaten off of it? What about your "good" sheets? Who are you saving them for? And exactly how many expensive, scented candles do you own that have never seen a match?

Squirrelling away your beautiful things for a day when you can justify indulging yourself is stupid. I'm going to guess you were given many of those items as gifts. (Let's face it; we don't usually buy ourselves nice things. We settle for the stuff in the clearance bin.) Did the giver expect you to stash the gift in a closet until you were worthy of using it? You need to assume the gift was presented because the giver felt you were worthy of using it— from the moment it was given, not to be saved until some arbitrary, future date.

Deprivation is a form of punishment. Self-deprivation is masochistic. I get it; you're not perfect. But neither is anyone else. Being kind to yourself makes you more inclined to be kind to others. It becomes a motivation for paying it forward. If you can't indulge yourself for your own sake, maybe it's time to get with a little self-love for the sake of everyone else in your life. So let's get started.

I'm going to guess that somewhere in your house, you have a nice set of dishes. It's a rite of womanly passage to get a lovely set of dishes when setting up a first home. So why are you relegating yourself and your family to the chipped, mis-matched, beat-up dinner plates you've had since the Year One when you have a lovely set hiding in a china cabinet? What's that? Because they respect nothing and will have the things broken inside of a week? Oh. Okay. That I can understand.

Lots of times, we rationalize keeping our precious things "for good" because we know that daily life is rough. Daily life beats people up. And it beats up our stuff as well. So our rationale is to hide the good stuff. Save it for a day when everything's perfect and we can set the table with the beautiful embroidered cloth, gently place the delicate china on top, drink from the crystal glassware, consume the perfect meal and that evening, retire to our beds to sleep on the Egyptian cotton sheets that, as of the moment, are still in the package.

So…exactly how often to you expect that day to manifest itself? That's right—NEVER. Which leads us back to the hoarding. Which means you'll never get to use your special things, right? Wrong.

There is a compromise. At least once a week, preferably when you're alone and can appreciate the moment, head over to the china cabinet and take out one of those beautiful dishes. Put it on a placemat or lovely tablecloth (also hidden in some drawer), and lay next to it a MATCHING set of utensils—along with a cloth napkin, if possible. Take a crystal glass from the dining room, in fact, sit in the dining room, and use your good dishes to eat an everyday meal.

Who deserves this treat more than you? Who will appreciate it more than you? Who, in your household, will appreciate it *besides* you? Right, probably no one, which is all the more reason for you to indulge yourself, by yourself.

While you're at it, indulge in a little fantasy as well. Imagine you're worth all of this special treatment. Wait a minute—you are.

Since the beginning of time, when we were pegged as the damnation of the human race (Remember Eve and that whole apple thing?) we women have never thought we were worth the good stuff. So we relegate ourselves to saving our beautiful things for other people, but never ourselves. I mean, if you're the damnation of mankind, how could you possibly deserve to eat off the good dishes?

Food is one of the joys of life. Too often, we women nourish ourselves with the aforementioned burnt toast and bread crusts while standing at the kitchen sink and signing a permission slip or writing a check or compiling a grocery list. Sitting at a lovely table savoring a meal (or even a p.b. & j., as long as it's on a china plate) is a soul-soothing ritual worthy of an idol. Worthy of you.

Now, what's going on in your bedroom? Of course you don't want to actually wear Granny Panties in the bedroom, but that's not what we're talking about. Your bedroom is supposed to be a sanctuary—for you to rest and rejuvenate yourself. The room, and your bed, should be luxurious. Okay, maybe you can't afford luxurious. But I'm willing to bet you could afford to at least buy a new set of sheets, one without holes and stretched out elastic. Exactly how old are the sheets you're sleeping on? Can you measure the age in dog years? Buy some new sheets. And if you're hiding a nice set in your closet, for heaven's sake, put them on the bed.

When you turn down the blankets at night, take a moment to feel your new sheets. Realize that the person about to climb into that bed has fought the good fight for yet another day and has earned a little pampering. Then, slather some lovely lavender-scented lotion on your hands from the recently purchased bottle you are now keeping next to your bed, slip in between the covers, close your eyes and imagine you're drifting off in Cinderella's castle—and someone else is in charge until the next day. (Use ear plugs and a sleep mask to block out the nocturnal wanderings of adult children if you must. Cinderella needs, and deserves, her beauty sleep.)

Okay, now it's time for a poll. How many pricey, designer candles do you have hidden in a cabinet somewhere in the house? Five? Ten? More?

I have "more." I won't say how many more. Suffice it to say that when I walk into the Yankee Candle store, they call me by my first name and ask about my husband and kids.

A number of years ago, a thoughtful friend gifted me with a wonderful scented candle at Christmas. Given that Christmas is a season of excess and I was feeling a bit self-indulgent, I lit it. Within minutes, the room was filled with a sweet, glorious smell that was positively transformative. Suddenly, the stresses of the season melted away and I felt—well, happy.

From that point on, I was hooked on the power of scent. It can calm, excite, even make you feel extravagant, minus the price tag. (Sure, some candle prices cause sticker shock, but if you figure that a $25 candle can give you over 150 hours of relaxation, it works out to around 17 cents an hour —a bargain.) And I'm willing to bet you have at least one candle in the house that you're saving "for good" which has yet to feel the heat of a match. Guess what? You're good enough. Light the damn thing.

Here's an added benefit. Everyone looks better in candle light. Everyone. So you might consider lighting one of those delightful scented candles you have stashed in the cabinet in the living room and heading up to your bedroom, where you dim the lights and settle in on a clean, crisp, new set of sheets. The perfume of the candle will relax you, while the soft lighting will make everything, including you, look luminous. Of course, what you do after that is your business, but I'm pretty sure it won't involve Granny Panties.

There are likely at least a dozen things right in your own home that you can immediately take ownership of to make your life better. Not "Yay! All my problems are solved" better, but "Hey, I feel pretty good right now" better. Treating yourself to the good dishes, new sheets or a candle indicates that you believe you have value. And if you don't believe it, no one else will, so get with it.

While your own home is the perfect place to begin your self-indulgence, the outside world holds lovely, accessible treasures as well. A little gift for you doesn't have to be expensive and you'll be amazed at how a small treat once a week makes you feel special.

One idea—fresh flowers. Once a week, or once a month or every other month, pick up a bouquet of fresh flowers. You don't even have to set foot in a flower shop; pick them up at the grocery store. (But you should set foot in a flower shop; it's a glorious experience.) A five dollar bunch of carnations (eight bucks will get you a few lilies and a rose or two) will do wonders to lift your spirits. Or, buy a new lipstick. Get a manicure or just purchase a new nail polish. Stop at a candy shop and pick up a quarter pound of a dark chocolate treat. Buy yourself a fashion magazine and picture yourself on the arm of George Clooney.

Again, it's not about the price of the item; it's about the price you assign to yourself. You don't have to spend a mortgage payment on a treat. Just believe that you are worthy of it. Then, even a three dollar lipstick will satisfy.

Perhaps the most important way to indulge yourself, though, and what is at the heart of everything we've just discussed, is time. Time spent on you and only you. Whether it's a morning ritual during which you enjoy a cup of coffee or tea and read the paper before you start the day's madness or a twenty minute yoga workout at the day's end or a half-hour dose of *Say Yes to the Dress* before you start cooking dinner, it's essential that you allot some of the day's 24 hours to you.

No one in your house deserves it more or needs it more. And no one will benefit from it more. Actually, everyone around you will benefit, as being good to yourself will keep you from regularly curling up into a fetal position and crying yourself to sleep.

If you can't find a fifteen minute block of time (and there are days when finding ten minutes to use the bathroom is a challenge), grab five minutes. Sit in your car at the grocery store and before you go in, push the buttons on the radio until you find a song you like and listen to it. All of it. Sing along if you want. But take the three and a half minutes, close your eyes and forget that you're about to get in line behind some jerk in the express lane who has forty items in his cart and is paying with a check.

The details aren't important. What is important is that you take some time, each and every day, to appreciate yourself. Treat yourself like the Cinderella you are. Idolize yourself. By doing so, you'll not only feel better, you'll inspire those around you to treat you better, too. You'll find yourself treating others better as well. You are worthy of idol worship. And by placing that imaginary tiara on your head, you'll move miles away from those nasty Granny Panties.

Live now. Enjoy now. Treat yourself—to both lovely things and time—now. Self-indulgence isn't selfish; it's essential to a healthy life. Remember what you've given to your world and those around you. Remember how much it's cost you to get to this point. Remember just how wonderful you are and worship yourself, just a little, every single day.

Then, once and for all, you can kiss those Granny Panties goodbye.

Try This!

Canvass all of the cabinets, drawers and closets in your home where you've hidden away the lovely items you're "saving for good." Use the lines below to make a list of every item. Then, choose three things and begin using them in your home immediately. Work your way through the list until you've treated yourself to using each item at least once. Finally, make sure each item is placed into regular, useful rotation in your daily life.

_____

_____

_____

_____

_____

_____

_____

Make a list of a five small indulgences you'd enjoy (i.e. flowers, dark chocolate). Then, once a week, treat yourself to an item on the list. Add to the list as you think of more things and be sure to treat yourself to a little gift every week!

_____

_____

_____

_____

_____

_____

_____

_____

_____

_____

_____

_____

_____

Congratulations! If you have completed all of the exercises in this book and resolved to keep the commandments, you can now live your life free of Granny Panties.
But before you go eat some chocolate and contemplate your own amazingness, keep reading for the final word....

Epilogue

Sometimes, when I look in the mirror (and my underwear drawer), I miss my youth. I miss the carefree teenage years. Then I miss my early twenties, when I had only myself to think about. Then I miss my thirties, when the kids were young and I thought I finally had life figured out.

And then I remember what all of that was really like.

As I recall, I spent approximately seventy-five percent of the years between thirteen and nineteen in tears. During my twenties, I did not have only myself to think about, having married at the ridiculously young age of twenty-two. I worried constantly about money, marriage and career. Once my thirties came along, I was three kids in, a neurotic, frazzled mother trying to juggle everybody's everything and losing myself and my mind in the process.

Youth, though it can be wonderful, can also be seriously overrated. And while there is a risk that as we age, we can get stuck in a pinching, bunching pair of Granny Panties, I'll take this point in my life. In fact, I embrace it.

I don't embrace the wrinkles, or the sags and bags, aches and pains and so on. But I am thrilled that I can finally, without fear of legal retribution, tell my kids to figure things out for themselves. In fact, now that we've crossed that bridge, we've developed more pleasant relationships; sometimes, we even enjoy each other.

I'm also thrilled that my husband and I are finally getting to the point where we can spend some time together, in an effort to recall just what it was we saw in each other in the first place. We're remembering that we actually enjoy each other's company, now that our conversations have progressed beyond a daily synchronization of schedules and barking of orders.

And I'm happy that as more and more time passes, I care less and less, mostly about what people think of me. There's a contentment, a freedom that comes with not giving a crap about what anyone else thinks, and I'm loving it.

While some of this has been a natural by-product of early senility (if you don't remember stuff, it's easy not to care about it), making peace with life's middle ground isn't a given. In truth, it takes work to steer clear of the Granny Panties that are ready and waiting for us as we move forward. It takes commitment, to valuing yourself and what you've accomplished in your life so far, whether your greatest achievement to date is performing brain surgery or raising kids who aren't in jail and not strangling your mother when she asks what you did to your hair.

Avoiding Granny Panties is really about living. It's about remembering what you enjoy and finding a way to do it. It's about forgetting what no longer matters and ignoring life's minor annoyances. Staying out of Granny Panties occasionally means giving up control and giving in to the moment. And saying "No" once in a while. It's passing up the urge to check out a mirror, but only after you've made yourself presentable by tossing out the puppy shirts, elastic-waist pants and gym shoes.

Passing on Granny Panties means passing on what you "should" be doing and taking a chance on doing something that scares the hell out of you. Or accessing your inner six-year-old and blowing some bubbles. It's about being a "bad" girl once in a while and slipping your Cinderella feet into a pair of red high heels.

And finally, it's about idolizing yourself, assigning yourself a value that allows you to eat off of the good dishes, light a scented candle even though you're alone or watch the Food Network for an entire day without ever planning to cook a single recipe, while polishing off an entire bag of Doritos in the process.

You are fabulous. You are worth it. Carpe diem. It's all you've got. So live well, be well, be happy, and remember: No one, and I mean no one, looks good in Granny Panties. So keep the commandments.

As for the Granny Panties?

Toss 'em. Toss 'em hard, toss 'em far, and don't *ever* look back.

ABOUT THE AUTHOR

MARY FRAN BONTEMPO is an author, teacher and speaker who writes with humor and insight about the lives of women, especially as they journey through life's various phases. Her first book, *Everyday Adventures or, As My Husband Says, "Lies, Lies and More Lies,"* chronicles her adventures in modern-day womanhood. Her work has won numerous awards, including notable mention by the Erma Bombeck Writer's Workshop and Humor Press. She currently writes for her blog, *Not Ready For Granny Panties* (www.notreadyforgrannypanties.com), and Technorati Media.

ABOUT THE ILLUSTRATOR

PAT ACHILLES is, in her own words, the anti-artist: too chubby to be edgy, too realistic to be abstract, and too easily distracted to be intense. Pat maintains a sense of fun in her drawings and so far, hasn't found a subject she can't illustrate with skill and humor, including theatrical posters, caricatures, floral catalogues, children's books, logos, custom cards, etc. To see more of Pat's work, go to www.achillesportfolio.com.

CPSIA information can be obtained at www.ICGtesting.com
Printed in the USA
BVOW03s0819060914

365337BV00001B/1/P

9 781456 609290